IMAGES
of America

SAN FRANCISCO'S GLEN PARK AND DIAMOND HEIGHTS

After the 1906 earthquake, hundreds of temporary shacks were built in Glen Canyon to house the refugees. (Glen Park suffered little damage.) Many of the displaced San Franciscans were charmed by the hills and views and decided to stay. At least half a dozen shacks were moved into the neighborhood and converted into tiny homes. (Courtesy San Francisco Public Library.)

ON THE COVER: In the fall of 1906, a few months after the great earthquake, Glen Park was just beginning to grow as a neighborhood. Residents began to form clubs as a means of socializing and creating community spirit. Here members of the Glenora Social Club pose on the old Bosworth road at Hamerton Avenue. There is very little information about them, but dances, "moonlight picnics" in the park, and parades were probably a few of their activities. In the photograph, the dirt road in the background is Chenery Street, near where St. John's School is today. The rails for the Dinky Line streetcar are just in front of the wagon. (Courtesy private collector.)

IMAGES
of America

SAN FRANCISCO'S GLEN PARK AND DIAMOND HEIGHTS

Emma Bland Smith

ARCADIA
PUBLISHING

Published by Arcadia Publishing
Charleston, South Carolina

Library of Congress Catalog Card Number: 2007920163

For all general information contact Arcadia Publishing at:
Telephone 843-853-2070
Fax 843-853-0044
E-mail sales@arcadiapublishing.com
For customer service and orders:
Toll-Free 1-888-313-2665

Visit us on the Internet at www.arcadiapublishing.com

In 1950, most of Glen Park was already built up, but there have been some changes since. BART and 280, for instance, had not yet gone in, and here one can see the blocks of houses that were demolished for the construction. Martha Hill (now Dorothy Erskine Park) sits in the center of the photograph, and San Jose Avenue runs horizontally across the top. Visually, the greatest change has been the growth of trees. (Courtesy San Francisco Redevelopment Agency.)

CONTENTS

Acknowledgments   6

Introduction   7

1.   Before the Earthquake   9

2.   An Outside Land No Longer   23

3.   The Business District   45

4.   The Bernal Cut and San Jose Avenue   61

5.   Bosworth, O'Shaughnessy, 280, and the Freeway Revolts   73

6.   The Fairmount Tract   87

7.   A Real Neighborhood: Schools, Parks, and Churches   99

8.   Diamond Heights   111

ACKNOWLEDGMENTS

I will never again look at the streets and houses of Glen Park in the same way. Although this book is not a comprehensive, nor an authoritative, text, I hope that the pictures and stories it contains will make old Glen Park come alive for readers, the way they did for me. Collecting the photographs, maps, and information was a challenge, and I have to thank all the people who contributed to my project. Special thanks, first of all, to Greg Gaar for opening up his photograph collection to me. Valerie Chester Hoover, Cathie Schafer, and Joan Strachan went out of their ways to dig through family albums and city records. Fellow Arcadia authors Richard Brandi, Emiliano Echevarria, Jacquie Proctor, Jack Tillmany, Lorri Ungaretti, and Bill Yenne shared advice and images. Dawn Murayama took me on a personalized Glen Park walking tour. Michael Waldstein took gorgeous pictures of the business district. Marie Browning at the San Francisco Redevelopment Agency was incredibly kind and welcoming. Others whose aid was invaluable include the following: Jack Coll, Ron and Joanne Davis, Joy Durighello, Patricia Duff, Dolan Eargle, Bill Ingraham, Dan Gustavson, Ken and Kathy Hoegger, Steve Kearns, Woody LaBounty, Zoanne Nordstrom, Daniel Oppenheim, Jane Radcliffe, David and Lea Schermerhorn, Buck and Turk Tergis, Christina Trost, Christopher VerPlanck, Bonnee Waldstein, Elizabeth Weise, Larry Wisch, and Stuart and Shannon Wren. Thanks to John Poultney for his guidance, and to my family and friends who helped take care of Everett so I could work. And thanks to little Everett, the next generation.

INTRODUCTION

What makes Glen Park and Diamond Heights stand out from many other San Francisco neighborhoods today? More than anything else, it's the topography. Most streets are built on a grade, and there's always a hill in the background. Look this way, and you see the triplets of Fairmount, Red Rock, and Gold Mine; that way, Mount Davidson looms; over in the corner, if you lean far enough, you will glimpse Bernal Heights or Twin Peaks. And unlike more iconic hilly areas such as North Beach or Russian Hill, some of Glen Park's peaks and valleys have remained undeveloped and wild. The wild and beautiful Glen Canyon Park is possibly the crown jewel in San Francisco's parks department.

How many urban enclaves have their own river? It's ironic that few people who live here today are familiar with Islais Creek, since this small rushing stream, which starts above the canyon near Portola, runs through the canyon and joins the bay near Hunter's Point and has been, until recently, a significant feature of the neighborhood. For thousands of years before the arrival of the Spanish and Mexicans in California, the Ohlone Indians lived here. In the 1800s, Mexican ranchers, then European dairy farmers, grazed their cows in the canyon. The creek powered the boilers for the generators of the first electric streetcars in the 1890s, and businesses such as the tannery, located on Bosworth Street near Arlington Street, depended on the water as well.

Islais Creek may be the reason the first settlers chose to come here, but later, Glen Park's steep hills hemmed it in and made it too remote for most people to consider living in it. The city that had 450 inhabitants in 1848 and 20,000 in 1849 had almost 300,000 by 1890, but Glen Park was still part of what San Franciscans called the Outside Lands. To tell its history is to talk about imagination, ambition, and private enterprise. A German immigrant named Behrend Joost changed the future of the neighborhood when he brought rails to Glen Park. Joost organized the first electric streetcars, running down Chenery Street, Diamond Street, and Monterey Boulevard, making the neighborhood a much more practical place to settle.

Glen Park is a place that often falls under the radar of even lifelong San Franciscans. We spiral down O'Shaughnessy, pick up and drop off at the BART station, enter the freeway at Monterey, hike in Glen Canyon, shop at the Diamond Heights Safeway, and take classes at City College, unaware that a tight-knit community with a rich history has existed right off the beaten path for just about 100 years now.

Much of Glen Park's charm derives from its slightly askew, half-country atmosphere. Glen Park's boundaries run along San Jose Boulevard to the east, then west along Thirtieth Street to Diamond Heights Boulevard, north to Portola Drive, west along Portola then south down O'Shaughnessy Boulevard, cutting along the Sunnyside District around Joost Avenue, and back to San Jose Avenue. The neighborhood feels—and is—less "planned" than many other parts of San Francisco. Many of Noe Valley's streets were intended to run right through, but only two of them show up today—and with a big gap. If you find Castro on a Glen Park map, then trace it northeast to Noe Valley, you will see that they would have connected if not for the hills. Diamond Street's two portions almost meet; just the ridge of the hill separates them. In the area of Glen

Park just east of the canyon, one would be hard pressed to find a standard, four-way, right angle intersection. Some streets are as short as a block, some are partially unpaved. Many run diagonally, or turn unexpectedly. Quite a few corner houses are triangular, and some are set back or at an angle from the curb, built before the streets were graded. The architecture changes from house to house, from shingled cottage to Victorian beauty to rustic farmhouse, reflecting the diverse backgrounds and tastes of the immigrants who were making Glen Park their new home.

In her book *The Last Mexican Alcade of Yerba Buena: Jose de Jesus Noe* (1991), Mae Silver warns against looking at history from the white European viewpoint alone. Long before the first farmhouse was built in the canyon, Jose Noe owned all of what is today Glen Park. Silver captures the romance of Mexican San Francisco in her own verse:

> This is the soil he knew.
> These streets were his trails.
> The hills covered with houses
> Were grass for his cattle.
> Vegetables grew in the valleys
> And orchards marched alongside.
> He watched the world blanket the Bay
> From the top of Twin Peaks.
> He heard the Mission bell
> And children playing in the poppies.

On Friday nights, Glen Park comes alive with the sound of jazz from the Chuck Peterson Quintet wafting onto Diamond Street. Bird and Beckett Books, where they have played since 2002, has been a fixture in the neighborhood since 1999. Here, from left to right, Chuck Peterson, Don Prell, and Bill Perkins hone their art. (Courtesy Michael Waldstein.)

One

BEFORE THE EARTHQUAKE

The history of modern Glen Park has been written mostly by developers and major landowners. The timeline begins in 1839, when Jose de Jesus Noe (1805–1862), the last mayor of the city under Mexican jurisdiction (when it went by the name Yerba Buena), acquired a huge plot of land called Rancho San Miguel. Sprawling over one-sixth of the city, the 4,443-acre rancho included today's Noe Valley, Castro, Glen Park, Twin Peaks, Diamond Heights, Midtown Terrace, West Portal, St. Francis Wood, and Forest Hill. Noe grazed his cattle over this land but did not develop it more than that. It passed through several other owners until it was bought by Adolph Sutro in 1880. This former mayor, who once owned one-twelfth of the city, left a legacy in the form of the eucalyptus trees that cover Mount Sutro and Glen Canyon (naming the former Gum Tree Ranch), but likewise, did not develop it significantly.

Then, in the 1890s, developers began buying up the land around Glen Park. The Crocker Estate had a real estate company and was San Francisco's biggest landholder, owning most of what is now Glen Park; they famously started a zoo and small amusement park in the canyon to attract potential buyers. Equally ambitious were three German brothers named Behrend, Isaac, and Fabian Joost, who owned some of Glen Park and much of neighboring Sunnyside. Realizing that without public transit no one could reasonably live here and commute to jobs downtown, the brothers founded the city's first electric streetcar line, running from Market Street all the way to Daly City via Chenery Street and San Jose Avenue.

The skeleton of a neighborhood now existed, but real estate sales would not really take off until after the 1906 earthquake. For the last decade of the 19th century, Glen Park remained Little Switzerland: a hilly, scenic area inhabited by farmers, perfect for day trips and picnics in the canyon but too remote for most to live there.

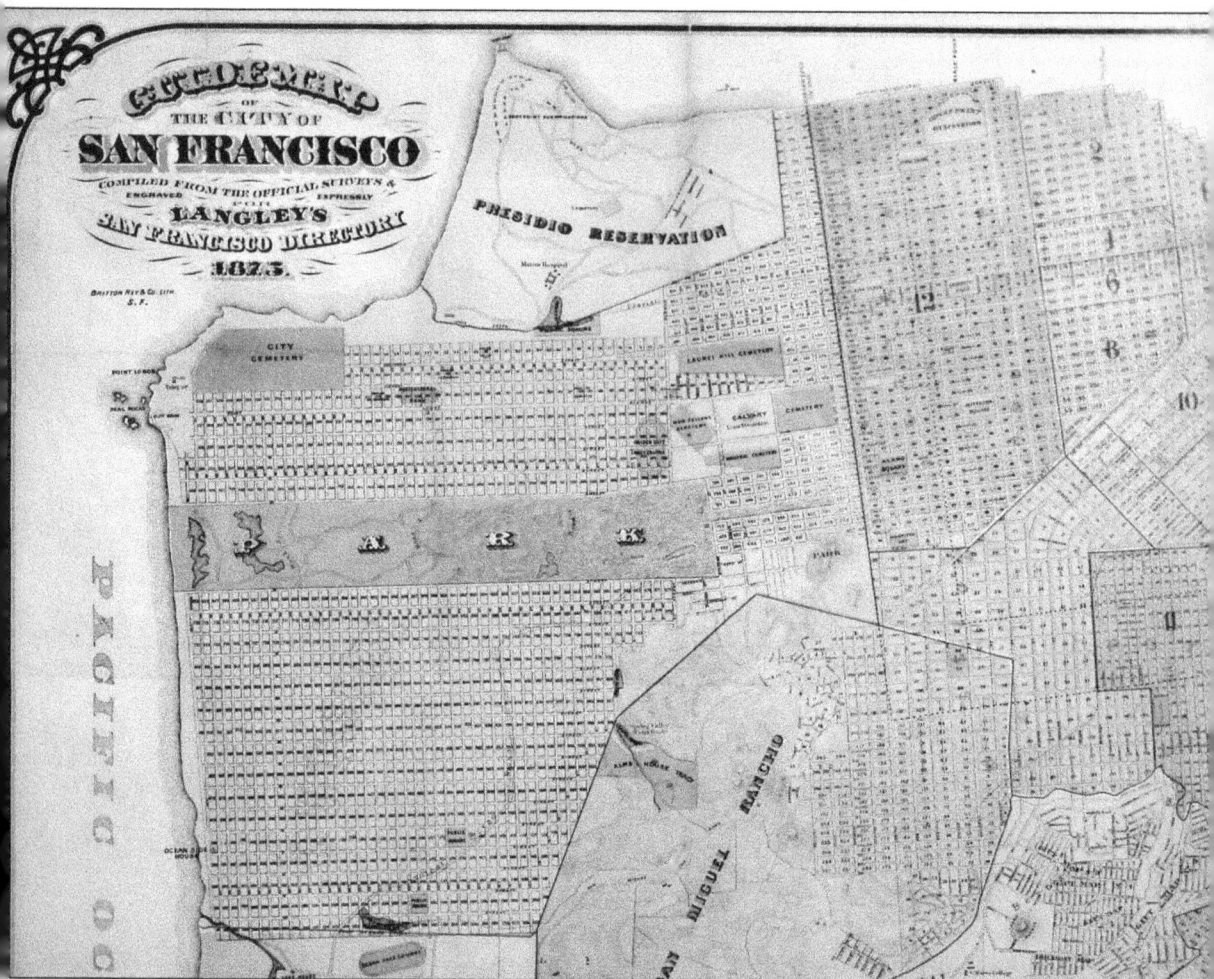

Rancho San Miguel is in the geographic center of the city. By 1873, it had already changed hands several times, from Jose Noe to John Horner in 1852, to partners Pioche and Robinson a decade later, and finally to Adolph Sutro in 1880. Certain parts of the rancho, such as Noe Valley and the Fairmount Tract, were developed as early as the 1860s, but the western part of Glen Park was still home only to dairy and vegetable farmers and a variety of light industry (a basket factory, shoe factory, artificial flower factory, and tannery). Interestingly, in this map, Castro Street is drawn all the way through; developers soon realized the hills made that impossible, and today the two parts of Castro do not meet (and the same is true of Diamond Street). Note that while the entire Sunset District is plotted out here on a grid pattern, it was not built up until the first part of the 20th century. (Courtesy Dennis Minnick.)

In 1885, Adolph Sutro's sapling eucalyptus trees, though fast-growing, had yet to obscure the wide-open views and pastures. In this beautiful photograph, probably taken from the eastern slopes, one can see a German beer garden in the far distance (across from where the School of the Arts High School is now), where people would stop on their way to the Ingleside racetrack. Twin Peaks presides in the distance. (Courtesy private collector.)

Decades later, O'Shaughnessy Boulevard would wind its way along the rocky hills on the right side of this 1903 photograph. The small, pointed peak in the center of the photograph was called Columbine Incline, so named after the flowers that bloomed there. In winter months, water would course down this dry creek bed. (Courtesy private collector.)

In 1950, the depth of Glen Canyon was still largely as it had been for millennia, although during the construction of O'Shaughnessy Boulevard (completed in 1941), heaps of debris were dumped unceremoniously into the canyon. The houses on the right are part of Miraloma Park. One can see the beginning of Glen Park and the baseball field at top. (Courtesy San Francisco Redevelopment Agency.)

Glen Canyon, with the small but ancient Islais Creek, has always been a center of activity. For hundreds of thousands of years, elk, mountain lions, and grizzlies stopped to drink from the stream, as Greg Gaar and Ryder W. Miller write in their book, Images of America: San Francisco, A Natural History. Later the Ohlone Indians may have worked in the stream. While there are rumors of gold miners in Glen Canyon in the 1840s, the red Franciscan rock formation is not known to hide gold, so that is likely just a rumor. Later, in the 1860s, the Giant Gunpowder Factory built a plant in the canyon, but it exploded in 1869 and subsequently was banished. The creek bubbled on, running unharmed through San Francisco and emptying into the bay via Islais Creek Channel, near Hunter's Point. (Courtesy private collector.)

In the 1880s, Alfred Clarke (possibly the well-dressed figure in the foreground) dammed the creek and constructed a wooden pump house, with a power-generating boiler, to bring water to his waterworks on Kite Hill in Eureka Valley. Mount Davidson rises just to the left of this photograph. The stream was undammed years later. (Courtesy private collector.)

The pump house was located where the baseball field is today. The grove of eucalyptus trees in the distance (most of which are gone today) is the current location of the Chenery and Diamond Streets intersection. Wild irises grow in the meadow in the foreground. (Courtesy private collector.)

The canyon looks pristine in this 1880 shot, but dairy farms and ranches, despite their wholesome associations, were not without deleterious effects on the landscape. An 1893 sewer report states that the upper part of Islais Creek was "fouled by refuse from truck gardens, pig-pens and corrals." Today the creek and canyon are kept clean by the Friends of Glen Canyon Park, headed by Richard Craib. (Courtesy private collector.)

The canyon was recently declared one of the city's six "Significant Natural Resource Areas." Volunteers work to maintain its wild quality and restore some of its original vegetation and animal habitat while making it a special place to hike and enjoy the silence. Although the creek is 4 miles long in all, it is above ground for only 1 mile along the canyon floor. (Courtesy author.)

Before the discovery of gold, in the days of the Mexican ranchos, cattle raising had been San Francisco's primary source of revenue. After the Gold Rush, when the village of Yerba Buena went from 450 inhabitants to 20,000 in two years, other industries sprang up, but dairies continued to exist. Cows need water, and the first grazing area was Washerwoman's Lagoon, in the Marina District. After a cholera epidemic caused by polluted drinking water, the herds were sent off to other areas, including Visitacion Valley and Glen Park. This photograph was taken in 1903 and captures the serenity and grandeur of the canyon. (Courtesy private collector.)

The Good Brothers Dairy remains the most fondly remembered business in Glen Canyon. Up through the 1940s, when the dairy closed, residents would walk down the path to buy milk for breakfast and whipping cream for dessert. Today the area where the dairy stands would be hard to see from this distance, due to the thick eucalyptus groves. (Courtesy Hal and Susan Tauber.)

Behrend Joost changed the course of Glen Park's future. Already a successful businessman and owner of a hardware shop on Mission Street, this ambitious young German immigrant was married to a woman named Anna Miller; they lived at 3224 Market Street in the home her father built, the first house on Twin Peaks and a historic landmark. Partnering with two of his three brothers, Joost decided to get into the real estate business. Gambling that the future of San Francisco was moving south, he bought up land west of Glen Park, optimistically named it Sunnyside, and began preparing to sell lots. (Courtesy Woody LaBounty.)

In the 1880s, however, it was still too time-consuming to get from downtown to this area, which was considered part of the Outside Lands. Residents had to walk to Mission Street and Cortland Avenue to catch horse-drawn transport. In 1890, the board of supervisors granted Joost the franchise to what would be the city's first electric streetcar line, the San Francisco and San Mateo line. (Courtesy private collector.)

16

GLEN PARK BRIDGE

Joost's streetcar started at the Ferry Building and made its way to Thirtieth Street and Chenery Street. Here riders would transfer to a larger car, which ran down to Diamond Street, turned left, and crossed a wooden trestle bridge (above) built the previous year to span Islais Creek. The streetcar carried on to Diamond Street and San Jose Avenue, all they way to Daly City. Another line took Monterey Boulevard to Gennessee Street. Unfortunately the line proved unable to single-handedly transform the neighborhood from farmland to bedroom community, and the Joost brothers lost money. The "Grand Old Man of Twin Peaks" and his brothers sold the railroad just three years after its debut, though they continued to deal real estate in the area and were ultimately instrumental in the development of Glen Park. (Courtesy Dan Gustavson.)

After the Joost brothers went bankrupt, the SF&SM changed hands several times. Portions were converted to bus lines in the early 1940s, and in 1944, they were bought by the Municipal Railway. The trestle was taken down around 1920, and the creek gulley filled in. This view looks down Diamond Street across the trestle toward Chenery Street. Most of the buildings still stand. (Courtesy Dan Gustavson.)

The Crocker Estate had bought much of Glen Park from Adolph Sutro in 1889 (the year of his death). To attract potential buyers to the neighborhood, which was now reachable by streetcar but had yet to really win civic respectability, one of the realtors working for Crocker, A. S. Baldwin, built a mini amusement park and zoo in the canyon, calling it the Mission Park and Zoo. This 1898 panorama of the opening-day picnic, looking east, shows a band playing on the bridge across Islais Creek. (The bottom photograph on page 13 has approximately the same perspective. Note the distant clump of eucalyptus trees in both shots.) San Franciscans flocked to the canyon on weekends for picnics and shows, though not necessarily to buy homes. (Courtesy private collector.)

A stereo photograph of the May Festival in the park shows a big barn at center, used for dances as well as for displays meant to hook home buyers (the real purpose of the zoo, after all). (Courtesy Ken and Kathy Hoegger.)

Rustic Walk around Lake.

A Lake on the Hill Top.

Mission Park & Zoo.

PICTURESQUE SAN FRANCISCO.

The Crocker park and zoo boasted bears, elephants, monkeys, and seals, plus an aviary, bowling alley, and hot air balloon rides. (Interestingly, the original seal tank still exists under a house on Hiliritas Avenue, on the eastern slope of Glen Canyon.) One of the greatest draws was a tightrope walker named Jimmy "Scarface" Williams, who walked across the canyon. (Courtesy private collector.)

PICTURESQUE SAN FRANCISCO.

Morro Castle, a miniature castle complete with moat, sat on the slopes of the canyon above the zoo and picnic grounds. In the panorama on page 18, one can spot it in the far left corner. (Courtesy private collector.)

1898

FRANCISCO DAILY REPORT: THURSDAY EVENING, SEPTEMBER 8

MORO CASTLE, GLEN PARK.

An Original and Unique Structure, which Will be Completed and Opened Tomorrow at the Mission Park and Zoo.

The Stars and Stripes will wave to-morrow over Morro Castle.

The event will be a joint celebration—the admission of California into the Union and the victory achieved by the "Report" and the people of the Mission in the gallant fight for a park in that district.

Every one who feels an interest in the development of the city, in the extension of its boulevards and its park system should go out to Glen Park tomorrow and see the site which the "Report" has been advocating for the Mission Zoo.

Morro Castle is one of the attractions of the new park. It is formidable in its outer aspect, but a visit to the interior will dispel any apprehensions the visitor may have.

Take your family out and let the children have a good time feeding the bunnies and guinea pigs in Morro Castle. Give them a day of pleasure on the children's playground, a ride on the donkeys.

The general invitation issued by the Mission Park Association reads as follows:

THE MISSION PARK ASSOCIATION

(the proposed Mission Zoo) on Admission Day, FRIDAY, SEPT. 9, 1898.

Note.—Take San Mateo Electric cars and get off at Chenery and Diamond streets, one of the entrances to the new Park.

MISSION PARK ASSOCIATION,
George D. Shadburne, Pres.
J. J. McEwen, Sec'y.

The occasion promises to be of historical interest. Among the distinguished gentlemen who have promised to be present is President David Starr Jordan of Stanford University who will presumably make a few appropriate remarks.

This 1898 newspaper article references the movement to beautify the city and create more extensive parks and grander boulevards. Highly regarded city planner Daniel Burnham was charged in 1904 with drawing up a plan for the entire city. His report was handed in just a few days before the earthquake; after April 18, 1906, the city was so busy scrambling to recover that few of his ideas were ever implemented. (Courtesy San Francisco Public Library History Room.)

20

Before the existence of the municipal railway, private streetcar lines were common. The Crocker Estate installed what locals called both the Dinky Line or the Toonerville Trolley, running from Mission Street along Bosworth Street to the zoo entrance at what is today Elk and Congo Streets. Regulars remembered Mr. Gates, the kindly operator, who would pass out candy to the kids. On Sundays only, a second line ran back and forth along Chenery Street between Diamond Street and the park. At this point, and until 1910 or so, the park was largely used by residents from other parts of the city for weekend excursions. The fare was 5¢. (Courtesy Ron and Joanne Davis.)

This 1900 map clearly shows the streetcar lines (the thicker dotted line traces the steam engine line). Note that the streets north of Chenery Street (which is not fully drawn here) are mapped out but still empty. At this time, the term "Glen Park" referred to the canyon itself, not to the neighborhood. (Courtesy Richard Brandi.)

It is very hard to imagine today, standing at the crossroads of Diamond Street and Chenery Street, the old timber trestle spanning Islais Creek. It is equally hard to conceive of a city with acres upon acres of wild, open space, where cows roamed and vistas revealed bare hills in all directions, or a place where a man could take it upon himself to start a railroad, build a bridge, and transform a neighborhood. And yet, that was Glen Park 100 years ago. (Courtesy Jack Tillmany.)

Two

AN OUTSIDE LAND NO LONGER

When the big quake leveled and burnt much of San Francisco on April 18, 1906, the army erected thousands of temporary refugee tents and shacks on the grasses of Glen Canyon, unknowingly shaping the future of the neighborhood. Many of the people who sought refuge in these shacks chose to remain in what was being marketed as Glen Park Terrace, buying lots at good prices from one of the city's biggest landholders, the Crocker Estate. One advertisement from November 1906 claims, rightly so, that "you'll probably never be able to buy a lot in San Francisco at $450 again—seize the opportunity now."

People flowed in. In 1880, one quarter of San Francisco's population had been Irish, but now immigrants from Germany, Scotland, Ireland, Sweden, Norway, England, and Italy began to arrive. (Many had already been living elsewhere in the city; the rustic peace of Glen Park appealed to them.) A school opened, corner stores dotted the streets, and beer flowed from German-style bars. Although Glen Park had no city services for some time and most streets were not paved until the 1920s, locals had vision to spare. They built a pipeline to carry in water, and they contributed $5 each a year to run a volunteer fire department, located at 2440 Diamond Street, with a horse-drawn engine.

The great variety of architectural style in Glen Park's houses reflects the diversity of its earliest residents. Rows of identical homes were generally built in one shot by a realtor. People with chickens or horses usually had a shed in the back, today often converted to a guest suite, studio, or garage. Very early houses were often set way back or at an angle, built before the streets were graded. And because of the hills, many homes in Glen Park are on multiple levels, or straddle two streets. The charm lies in the disorderliness of it all.

A succession of photographs taken from Martha Hill, south of Glen Park, shows the increasingly populated hills. Only the windswept, treeless peaks of Diamond Heights, where a few handfuls of farmers plied their trade, remained undeveloped. They, along with the mighty Mount Davidson, are the highly visible orientation points that grace the backgrounds of these old pictures.

After the April 18, 1906, quake, displaced San Franciscans waited in line on Arlington Street for supplies, distributed from a barn belonging to James Joseph Sullivan, whose father had settled in Glen Park in the 1880s and whose descendents still live here. The large white building in the background is the old Fairmount School at Chenery Street and Randall, built in the 1870s. The current building was erected in 1977. (Courtesy private collector.)

GLEN PARK TERRACE

On Guerrero-Street Electric Line

First Block of 40 Lots Entirely Sold Out

BY ORDER OF THE CROCKER ESTATE

We will offer another section of these
Choice Building Lots on the same

EASY TERMS

Lots $450 and $500 Each

Cottages at Actual Cost of Building

10 Per Cent Cash and $10 Per Month

AGENT ON GROUND SUNDAY

Take Ocean View or Guerrero-St. Cars and Get Off at Glen Park

G. H. UMBSEN & CO.

20 Montgomery Street

In 1906, the Crocker Estate owned most of what is now Glen Park. Although they had been trying to sell land for two decades, sales did not take off until after the earthquake, when many refugees housed in the canyon decided to stay. The agency G. H. Umbsen and Company worked for the Crocker Estate, selling lots at around $500 each. This advertisement appeared on October 21, 1906, in the *San Francisco Examiner*. (Courtesy San Francisco Public Library.)

Another Umbsen advertisement—this one from the November 18, 1906, issue of the *San Francisco Call*—explains the terms of the deal. Anywhere from $425 to $525 bought the lot; for $10 more a month, the sellers would build the landowner a cottage. According to this flyer, children were assigned to Sunnyside Grammar School; the Glen Park School on Lippard Avenue and Bosworth Street was built in 1910. Despite the "improvements" listed, most streets would remain unpaved for years, causing residents to complain about the dust in the summer and mud in the winter. (Courtesy San Francisco Public Library.)

These cottages at 52 and 54 Surrey Street are an example of the kind of pretty, peaked-roof homes that Umbsden was building for buyers. Today Glen Park is a very desirable neighborhood, with forbidding real estate prices that reflect that reputation. A century ago, however, it was being marketed almost exclusively to working-class people on affordable terms. (Courtesy Christopher VerPlanck.)

MAP OF
JOOST ADDITION
TO
GLEN PARK

Being a Subdivision of Blocks 9,10 and 11 of the
MISSION & 30TH STREET EXTENSION HOMESTEAD
SAN FRANCISCO

Scale 50ft to the inch

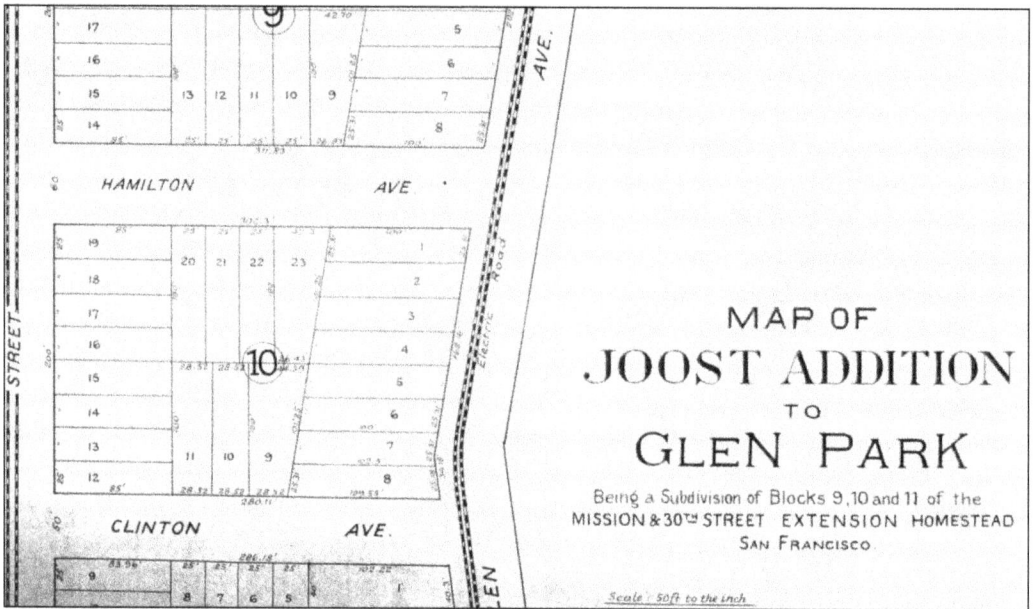

The enterprising Behrend Joost also had his foot in the Glen Park real estate world. He may not have made money off his railway, which he sold in 1896, but he had accomplished his real purpose—making Glen Park and Sunnyside easily accessible. On this July 1906 map, today's Chenery Street west of Diamond Street is called Glen Avenue, and Bosworth Street is Berkshire. (Courtesy Jane Radcliffe.)

FIRST ANNUAL PICNIC

GIVEN BY THE

Glen Park Improvement Association

SUNDAY SEPTEMBER 17, 1911

GAME PRIZES AND DANCING

Take Guerrero St. cars direct to grounds. Take Mission Street Cars and Transfer at Bosworth Street

TICKETS 25 cents   Children Under 12 Free   UNION MUSIC

A ROYAL GOOD TIME FOR ALL

Soon after the earthquake, residents formed the Glen Park Improvement Association. Members dug a pipeline to bring water to the neighborhood and organized a volunteer fire department, since the city did not service this area. Revived in 1997, the Glen Park Festival continues to take place every spring, at the crossroads of Chenery and Diamond Streets. (Courtesy Dan Gustavson.)

This 1919 photograph, taken on the 500 block of Bosworth Street between Diamond and Arlington Streets, looks north and shows the growth of Glen Park. The tank in the center was the John Honold Tannery (on Islais Creek), which closed down during Prohibition, when a raid produced a large bootleg still. The building on the extreme right was the Pacific Coast Basket Factory (at the intersection of Carrie and Wilder Streets). The horizontal street in the middle is Wilder Street, and Fairmount Hill towers are in the background. Today this block, right across from the BART station, is home to Glen Park Dental and a BART employees' parking lot. (Courtesy Ken and Kathy Hoegger.)

By 1914, the area was no longer called Rancho San Miguel; the term San Miguel Hills refers to the hills of Glen Park, Diamond Heights, and Mount Davidson. (Courtesy Richard Brandi.)

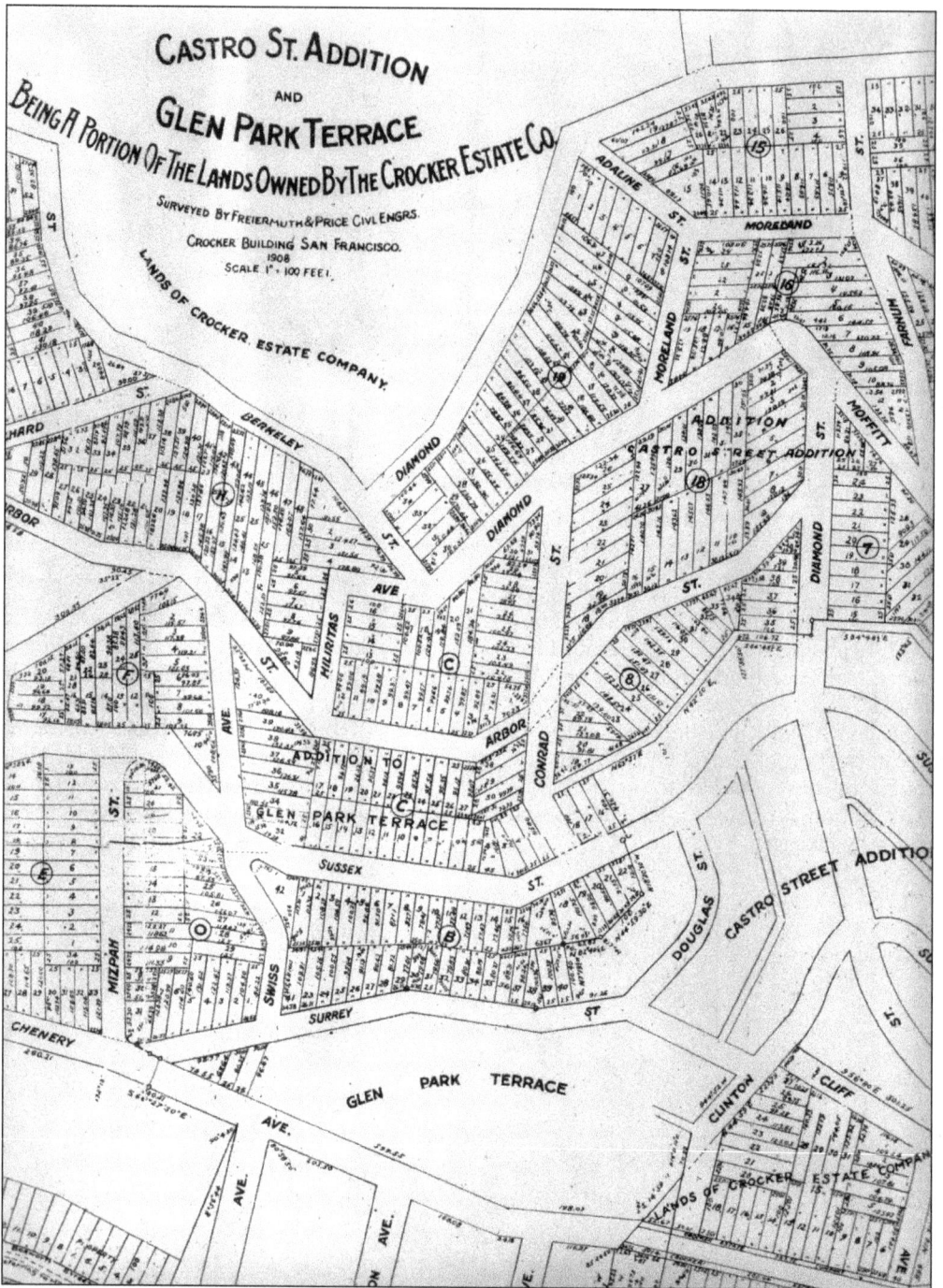

This 1908 real estate advertisement (continued on the following page) consisted of a detailed map showing every lot the Crocker Estate was selling. Since the lots on Bosworth Street and Chenery Street were owned by Behrend Joost, they do not show up on this map (but one can see them on the Joost map on page 26). Many of the lots in the southwest corner of this map are marked "sold," but the vast majority of the rest are still available, indicating that most Glen Park homes date from 1908 and after. (Courtesy Stuart and Shannon Wren.)

A close look at the map reveals that certain names have shifted and changed since 1908. Van Buren Street is called Douglas here, Ohlone Lane is unnamed (it was just a carriageway at the time), and Thor Avenue is Cliff. (Courtesy Stuart and Shannon Wren.)

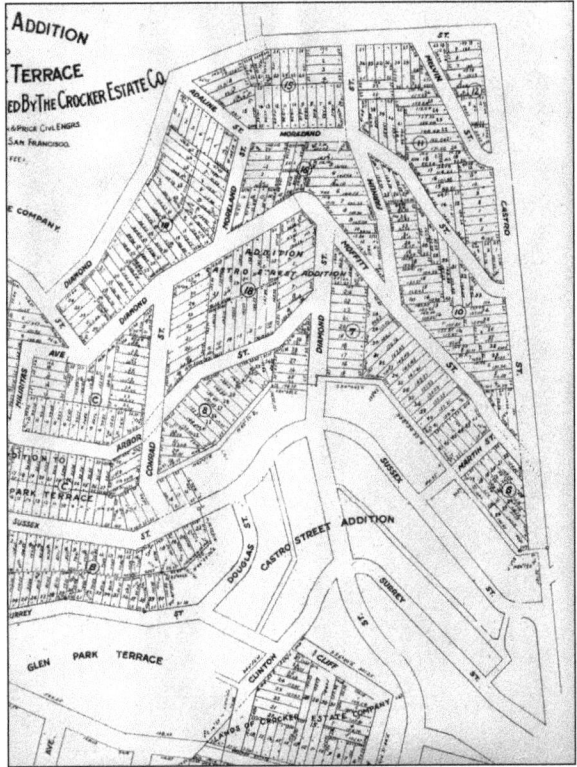

This advertisement represented Glen Park as a cross between St. Moritz and Hollywood. "The inevitable growth of San Francisco is to the south and southwest," trumpets the text. "Here, indeed, is the opportunity for the man of moderate means to acquire a home for his family on small monthly payments . . . on terms that must appeal to every thrifty, industrious person who wants to make a profitable investment." Lots were priced between $300 and $550. (Courtesy Stuart and Shannon Wren.)

A VERITABLE "SWITZERLAND"

If YOU have not visited this magnificent home residence park of "pine clad" splendor, with its regal parkings of imported shrubs, its wealth of semi-tropical bloom—you are missing, perhaps, the most phenomenal homesite opportunity you will ever have.

Not a mere real-estate tract, dotted here and there with a few "man made" beauty spots, to be used as advertising talking points—but a homesite where nature's deft fingers have wrought her handiwork.

Some amenities were available surprisingly early. The city water department keeps track of when houses were hooked up to running water, incidentally serving as a relatively reliable method of dating buildings. The home of saloon owner A. F. Dissmeyer, at 203 Surrey Street, was hooked up in 1895, but the architectural style of the house suggests it may date from earlier than that. Previously the family probably used a well in the backyard for their water supply. (Courtesy author.)

Running water was one thing, a sewer system was quite another, and came much later. This 1923 photograph, showing water mains being put in on Diamond Street south of Bosworth Street, is particularly poignant because all of the houses pictured were torn down in the 1960s; this is where the BART station is now. The Glen Park Branch Library was on this block before it moved to its Chenery Street location. (Courtesy Dan Gustavson.)

30

DAM SITE FOR THE PROPOSED SAN MIGUEL RESERVOIR, LOOKING DOWNSTREAM.
With camera set on point of rocks at east end of line B on contour map, with lens at about elevation 365.

In 1915, in the name of progress, a proposal was made to dam Glen Canyon and create a reservoir. Happily, the ill-conceived plan was never pursued to its conclusion. Today Glen Park gets its water from the College Hill reservoir, near Bernal Heights. (Courtesy private collector.)

A sweeping 1918 shot shows Islais Creek in the foreground and the Geneva carbarn in the center. Mount Davidson, on the left, slopes down to Red Rock, Gold Mine, and Fairmount Hills, with Glen Park beneath. The old 1901 carbarn, consisting of a wooden shed and a brick office building located at Geneva and San Jose Avenues, was a storage site for obsolete streetcars. It was closed in 1982 and the shed torn down by MUNI. For years, it seemed that the brick office building would suffer a similar fate, but in 1999, it was named a historical monument and is currently being restored for housing and office space. (Courtesy Ken and Kathy Hoegger.)

Public utilities slowly began to reach as far as Glen Park. This photograph of Sussex Street between Diamond and Castro Streets, with Gold Mine Hill in the distance, is from the city's telephone archives and documents technicians installing phone poles and wires. (Courtesy private collector.)

On February 24, 1911, men probably working on the San Francisco and San Jose Railroad line (where San Jose Avenue runs today) pose for a photograph. The imposing old Glen Park School is in the background at left. At right stands the distinctive Dissmeyer house, also pictured on page 30. (Courtesy Ken and Kathy Hoegger.)

Arlington Street gets electricity meters. In 1918, the western section of Glen Park's streets had not yet been paved; Arlington was considered part of the Fairmount Tract, an older part of town (developed in the 1860s like Noe Valley) that was modernized earlier. (Courtesy private collector.)

In the same shot today, the brown shingled house on the east side of the street is just barely visible, and all the empty lots have been filled in. (Courtesy author.)

Progress continued its march upon Glen Park. This photograph shows Mizaph Street in 1920, newly paved, looking north from Chenery Street toward Sussex Street, with the hills beyond still rural farmland. Just a few houses down Chenery Street toward Diamond Street, to the right of this photograph, exists an old storefront. Members of the Lucassen family operated it as a small market in the 1930s and 1940s. (Courtesy private collector.)

Some streets were never paved. Several alleys, including Penny, Poppy, and Ohlone Lanes, remain mostly dirt and grass to this day. They were originally carriageways for the houses on either side and were named sometime in the 1990s at the fire department's insistence. Here Penny Lane exudes a rustic, century-old ambience. (Courtesy author.)

Many homes were slightly altered when the streets were leveled and then paved. Around 1908, the house at 249 Whitney had at least nine steps, as this photograph indicates. Today it has only seven. (Courtesy Suzanne Sampson.)

The streets above Bosworth—Congo, Martha, and Stillings—were owned by the Crocker Estate and subdivided at the same time as their other Glen Park holdings (around 1908). They contain a number of charming early 1900s houses. This photograph from 1986 shows 37 and 45 Martha Avenue as they must have looked since 1911 and before remodling took place. No. 45 (right) was built by a German cabinet maker. There is a small neighborhood rumor that Stillings Avenue was named after an employee of a petting zoo and that Martha was his wife. (Courtesy author.)

3389. 30th & Chenery Sts. A.R. 295, 1-16-12.

This 1912 photograph looking up Chenery Street from Thirtieth Street toward central Glen Park was taken by Jesse Cook, a beat policeman and police commissioner who was also an amateur photographer. The track for the Nos. 10 and 26 streetcars comes west along Thirtieth Street then turns south down Chenery Street. Chenery Street goes slightly uphill for several blocks, and then at Roanoke Street, begins to slope downward. This downgrade was the cause of a number of runaway streetcar incidents in the first few years. As a car reached Diamond Street, if it had gathered up too much speed, it would occasionally fail to turn, jump the tracks, and plow into the businesses on the other side of Chenery Street. In 1894, the tracks were relaid and cars equipped with better brakes to fix the problem. (Courtesy private collector.)

After the Chenery Street portion, the No. 26 followed San Jose Avenue all the way to Daly City. The No. 10 took Monterey Boulevard to Gennessee Street, where it simply reversed its poles for the return trip. In the early 1940s, both lines was removed and replaced with diesel buses. Pictured here is the same Thirtieth Street and Chenery Street intersection in 1928. (Courtesy private collector.)

Today the J Church runs along Thirtieth Street past Chenery Street. Thirtieth Street is generally considered the dividing line between Glen Park (or the Fairmount Tract) and Noe Valley. (Courtesy Sally Bland.)

Glen Park continued to be an affordable option for self-starters wanting to buy a home and settle down. In 1934, Annie Lucassen poses in the backyard of her house at 2660 Diamond Street (the center house below). In the background is Diamond Street looking down toward Surrey Street. Annie and her husband, John, both German immigrants, bought the house and two adjacent vacant lots in 1927 and moved there with their eight children. (Left, courtesy Valerie Chester Hoover; below, courtesy author.)

Imelda "Mel" Lucassen, one of Annie and John's children, poses with her dog in Annie's backyard in 1934. Mel lived nearby on the corner of Chenery Street and Burnside Avenue, and owned a little grocery store at Chenery Street near Surrey Street. She later sold the store to her brother Edward and his wife, Muriel. (The storefront building is still there today, but no longer houses a grocery.) (Courtesy Valerie Chester Hoover.)

This wonderful 1938 photograph, taken from a rooftop on Surrey Street, shows the western side of Fairmount Hill. The little white house (58 Sussex Street), which is visible in all four photographs on these two pages, was the first home on the block. It is still there, though it has been greatly expanded. (Courtesy private collector.)

From approximately the same spot today, one can pick out the same lone white house, the third in the row in the top center of the photograph. The original peaked roof is now at the back of the structure; a second addition, including another rooftop, was added on later and is visible here. The lines of the hillside beyond, however, are completely hidden due to the remarkable tree growth. (Courtesy author.)

This *c.* 1935 photograph affords a sweeping panoramic view of Glen Park, with Fairmount Hill to the right and Gold Mine Hill rising to the left. The photographer was standing on Bosworth Street between Burnside and Hamerton Avenues, just a block from the school. Chenery Street runs horizontally in the middle of the photograph, and Lippard Avenue juts northward to the right. Today it would be very difficult to get the same view of Glen Park, because of the growth of the huge eucalyptus and pine trees along Bosworth Street. Bosworth Street was widened and made into a major thoroughfare in 1964, but here it is still a dusty unpaved road. (Courtesy private collector.)

Many a grand view of Glen Park, like this one from around 1935, was taken from Martha Hill. The row of six houses to the right (44–54 Surrey Street) was built by several brothers named Rivers in 1904. Like many early real estate buyers, the brothers may have been part of a homestead association, organizations that enabled people to pool their money to buy a chunk of land. They would then build houses and sell them off individually, like miniature housing tracts. (This is why there are so many rows of three or so identical houses all around San Francisco.) The distinctive peak of Bernal Hill is visible to the far right. (Courtesy private collector.)

This 1938 scene depicts a girl climbing among rubble in the backyard of a Diamond Street house. In the background one can make out Silver Avenue and the Excelsior District. (Courtesy private collector.)

Another photograph of Diamond Street, and the lone white house on Fairmount Hill, captures the simple working-class dignity of the neighborhood. This 1942 photograph was taken after a mud slide. (Courtesy private collector.)

A man poses on the grassy hills above Diamond Street in 1940. Beyond him rises Mount Davidson, the city's highest point (Twin Peaks are the second-highest), where development was crawling upward. In earlier photographs, Mount Davidson appears mostly bare; here its eucalyptus forest was beginning to take hold of the west side. The trademark cross stands at the very top of the mountain, and one curve of O'Shaughnessy Boulevard (completed in 1941) can be made out beneath the cliffs, behind a clump of trees. (Courtesy private collector.)

This 1945 photograph, also taken from Martha Hill, offers a clear view of Bosworth Street as a two-lane road. In 1964, the houses seen here on the north side were demolished to make way for the widening of Bosworth Street. Today the street has only a sidewalk on its north side, then drops off sharply to the Islais Creek ditch and Chenery Street. One of the buildings demolished was the old Glen Park library, at Bosworth Street and Brompton Avenue. At right is the current Glen Park School, built in 1935. (Courtesy San Francisco Public Library.)

Two lovely ladies (perhaps a girl and her mother?), *c.* 1910, kneel among the wildflowers of Martha Hill with the just-emerging Glen Park neighborhood for a backdrop. Chenery Street and Fairmount Hill are visible in the distance, and the six Rivers brothers' houses on Surrey Street are neatly framed by the trees. (Courtesy private collector.)

Three

THE BUSINESS DISTRICT

Before every family owned a car, Glen Parkers lived relatively contained lives and did most of their shopping and socializing within walking distance. The intersection of Chenery Street and Diamond Street was the heart of the neighborhood, home to butchers and bakeries, several ice cream parlors, a pharmacy, a five-and-dime, a hardware store, and even the Glenodeon movie theater, showing a different film every day for 10¢ each. Life had the flavor of a small village. Residents bought fresh fish from a man on a bike with a portable icebox. Another vendor peddled both coal and dead rabbits, and a newspaper boy stood on the corner shouting out the headlines.

Most important of all perhaps, to the hard-working men who needed a place to relax in the evenings, were the ever-present bars spilling copious amounts of beer. Dissmeyer's Saloon, on the corner of Diamond Street and Chenery Street and now occupied by Tyger's Coffee Shop, offered "sharp cool steam beer drawn direct from the keg" and was a fixture in the area from 1898 to 1920.

Corner stores, today a rare commodity, dotted the hills and were an even more vital part of the community than the bars. These small markets provided much more than groceries; owners kept tabs, gave credit, knew their clients by name, and delivered orders when people were ill. Sadly, most of the small corner markets are closed today, though one can peek into the past by walking along Chenery Street, Arlington Street, or Diamond Street looking for the many glass storefronts now converted to residences.

Glen Park in 1915 was still very much the frontier of San Francisco and exuded a dusty, Wild West ambiance. These two images come from the photo album of Val Tietz, member of a prominent early Glen Park family. They appear to be taken from the same location—possibly the back porch of the Tietz house at 657 Chenery Street. In the first shot, the streetcar rattles across the wooden Diamond Street trestle, over Islais Creek. Today the gulch has been filled in, and the houses at its bottom exist no longer. In the second picture, the photographer caught a spectacular view of the San Francisco and San Jose Railroad tearing down the Bernal Cut tracks, crossing Bosworth Street. The train would follow this route until 1928. (Courtesy private collector, San Francisco Public Library.)

The Tietz family built this magical little cottage, the neighborhood's oldest house, at 657 Chenery Street in 1872. The gabled cottage still stands, with entrances on both Chenery and Wilder Streets. John Tietz, a third-generation Glen Parker, also built the wooden building next door that housed the public library from 1964 to 2007. From left to right, the people with very German-sounding names posing here in 1909 are Cord Beneke, ? Mueller, Marie Mueller, Elise Beneke Tietz, Gesine Beneke, Kurt Beneke, and John Beneke. (Courtesy San Francisco Public Library.)

Elise Tietz was a widow (her husband worked on the railroad and was killed in a train accident) who supported her family tending cows and selling the milk all over Glen Park and the Fairmount Tract. Her son William married a woman named Val, from whose personal album come several photographs in this book. William and Val had a son John, who lived in the house at 657 Chenery Street. (Courtesy San Francisco Public Library.)

47

The crossroads of Diamond and Chenery Streets were the epicenter of Glen Park's business district. In this c. 1908 shot, the photographer was standing on the streetcar trestle on the corner of Bosworth Street, looking north up Diamond Street. Note the Umbsden realty sign advertising lots in Glen Park Terrace. The "witch's cap" building on the right remains an unofficial Glen Park landmark. (Courtesy Ron and Joanne Davis.)

Almost 20 years later, in 1937, the trestle is gone and the gulley has been filled in, making room for commercial development. A Safeway store stood where the new family-run grocery, Canyon Market, opened in fall of 2006. A big Bank of America was on the corner of Bosworth and Diamond Streets, where BART is now. (Courtesy Jack Tillmany.)

What is missing? One thing in particular has changed from 1937 to 1944: The tracks along Diamond Street and Chenery Street are gone, the streetcars having been replaced with diesel busses in 1942. This photograph is from the "Home Front" series in the *News Call Bulletin* during World War II. A Hancock gas station is to the right of the Safeway, which has lost its picturesque awnings. (Courtesy Dan Gustavson.)

The same view today is very much recognizable, the biggest difference being the development on the hills of Diamond Heights beyond. Canyon Market recently opened in the brick building on the right, and to the right of that (not in the photograph) is the brand new Glen Park Branch Library. (Courtesy Sally Bland.)

In the early 1900s, Chenery Street, near Diamond Street looking west toward the park, was barely recognizable, although the rails on the dirt road tip off the street's identity. A car is approaching the photographer, and a team of horses works to the right. Power lines are already in place. (Courtesy Ron and Joanne Davis.)

In 1939, the Purity market sat on the corner now occupied by Buddies Liquors. A current hangout, Tyger's Coffee Shop, was a drugstore in 1939, the cleaners was a five-and-dime, and a tavern was on the fourth corner (left). The building housing the five-and-dime is the oldest commercial structure in Glen Park and housed Straub's Saloon until the 1920s. (Courtesy Ken and Kathy Hoegger.)

In 1959, the rails are gone and the intersection looks very much like it does today. This is a peaceful shot, but in fact, 1959 was a year of turmoil for Glen Park. The city had just unveiled its plan to tear down over 100 homes to construct a major freeway along Bosworth Street and across Glen Canyon. Local activists were incensed and succeeded in shooting the plan down. (Courtesy Dan Gustavson.)

Today street trees planted by Friends of the Urban Forest give Glen Park a pleasant, leafy feel. A number of new businesses opened in 2006 and 2007, including Canyon Market, ensuring that the bustling village crossroads will continue to thrive. (Courtesy Sally Bland.)

As the pictures on this page attest, the dirt roads of Glen Park were anything but smooth. As automobiles became more common, the ruts must have become increasingly troublesome, and around 1918, paving began. (The stretch of Diamond Street between Chenery and Bosworth Streets was the first.) The houses in this *c.* 1910 photograph of Chenery Street between Lippard and Chilton Avenues, looking east, are still standing. Note the pretty, decorative painting on the houses to the left. (Courtesy Ron and Joanne Davis.)

In 1913, a little girl stands on Chenery Street near Castro (about where the old library stood), looking east. The road is severely rutted, there are no apparent sidewalks, and the streetcar is heading toward Thirtieth Street. This photograph is from the Val Tietz collection. (Courtesy private collector.)

These two photographs show the intersection of Chenery and Diamond Streets, looking east, in 1927 and in 2007. In the 1920s, the Higher Grounds café was a barbershop (owned by Irven Villmer), the hardware store was a grocery (owned by Martin and John Dierssen), Chenery Park was a butcher (owned by Daniel Little), and next door was another butcher (owned by Albert and Joseph Groebl). Across the street, the pet store was a barbershop (owned by Vincent Maita), No. 664 was another butcher (owned by Adolph Kratz), and No. 704—a beauty salon today—was yet another barbershop (owned by Arvid Asplund). Groebl's later became Vogel's meat market, a local favorite, where the friendly Albert Vogel handed out slices of bologna to kids. (Above, courtesy Sally Bland; below, courtesy private collector.)

Bars were big business in Glen Park, and there has been a saloon on every corner of Chenery and Diamond Streets. These men are posing outside a watering hole at Diamond and Wilder Streets. The spot was later occupied for 27 years by a bar called The Lodge, which later became the recently closed Red Rock, soon to reopen as a restaurant. (Courtesy Ron and Joanne Davis.)

In the 1940s and 1950s, a soda fountain and small grocery store operated at 732 Chenery Street. Like many small business owners, the Bagatelos family, from Greece, lived above their store; Vaneta and Peter's granddaughter, Karen Bagatelos, lives there today. After housing a bakery for 20 years, the storefront is now an architectural office. (Courtesy Karen Bagatelos.)

Before people had cars, they depended on corner stores for groceries and other necessities. The streetcar rumbled past quite a few small markets, including this one at Chenery and Fairmount Streets (photographed in 1938). Today the market is a home, and most of the other stores that used to dot the hills of Glen Park are no longer businesses. When people began to frequent supermarkets, with their lower prices and greater selection, smaller markets slowly disappeared, and today they are a rarity. (Courtesy Jack Tillmany.)

Another market, visible here at far left, with vintage checkered tiles, existed at the corner of Chenery and Roanoke Streets. This 1940 photograph was taken just two years before bad rail conditions caused the city to replace the streetcars with busses. (Courtesy Jack Tillmany.)

Many of the shop or saloon owners lived in the neighborhood, ran their businesses for many years, and were local characters with big personalities. Two such characters were Augustus Straub (above on Chenery Street in 1910), who ran a bar from 1898 to the 1920s in the spot where the cleaners is today, and A. F. Dissmeyer (below), who kept a lively saloon on the corner of Chenery Street where Tyger's Coffee Shop stands today. (Courtesy private collector and San Francisco Public Library.)

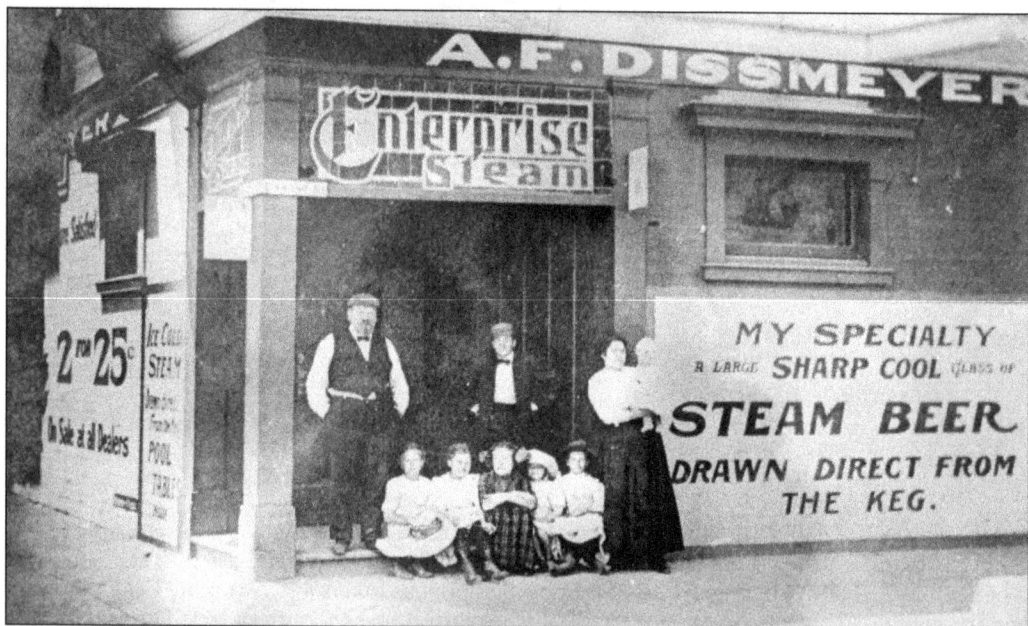

Glen Park continues to hum with activity. Rachid and Nada Malouf have owned the Cheese Boutique at 666 Chenery Street for 15 years. (Their other location in the Inner Sunset is 20 years old this year.) Besides the cheese selection and service with a smile, locals know there is no better source for homemade hummus and babaganoush. (Courtesy Michael Waldstein.)

Across the street, Chenery Park has been one of the neighborhood's culinary hot spots since 2000. Here general manager Joe Kowal, who lives in neighboring Sunnyside, gathers with the Moto Mêlée, an organization for vintage motorcycle enthusiasts who rent out the restaurant every year (a co-owner is a member). (Courtesy Michael Waldstein.)

In this late 1930s photograph, Edward Lucassen approaches the attendant at the Associated gas station to take the keys of his 1936 Plymouth. The new library is just to the left of where this gas station was, on Diamond Street between Wilder and Bosworth Streets. The next block of Diamond Street, between Bosworth Street and San Jose Avenue, housed a big Bank of America and the public library. Both were taken out when the freeway and BART went in. (Courtesy John Lucassen.)

The now-legendary Mitchell's Ice Cream at 688 San Jose Avenue (at Twenty-ninth Street) is a bit removed from the heart of Glen Park but is technically just a few blocks from the boundary. Fairmount residents in particular would have walked to Mitchell's, founded in 1953, for its dozens of homemade flavors. Beginning in 1860, the owners' grandparents, Edward and Margaret Mitchell, ran a dairy on Twenty-ninth Street in Noe Valley and grazed their cows on nearby Red Rock Hill. (Courtesy Mitchell family.)

Like all neighborhoods in the first half of the previous century, Glen Park had its own movie theater. The Glenodeon (a play on the word nickelodeon, the name for early theaters, so-called because admission cost a nickel) opened at 2780 Diamond Street in 1913. Its name changed to the Diamond in 1917 and so remained until it closed in 1929, just when "talkies" were making their debut. Here a crowd poses outside the theater in front of a poster for *Quincy Adams Sawyer*, a film released in 1922. (Courtesy San Francisco Public Library.)

Even in 1913, the 5¢ admission was affordable (though according to this program, five years later it was up to 10¢), and people enjoyed the movies far more frequently than today. (One source estimates that in 1907, two million people nationwide attended the nickelodeons daily.) The closure of the theater was a loss to the neighborhood, as the nearest other theaters would have been at Twenty-ninth and Mission Streets or Twenty-eighth and Church Streets. Nickelodeons often showed a series of short dramas, comedies, and "educationals." (Courtesy San Francisco Public Library.)

Diamond Theatre

2780 DIAMOND STREET

Adults 10c Children 5c · War Tax, 1 Cent · Evenings 7:15 and 8:45	PROGRAM FOR SEPTEMBER, 1918		SUNDAYS and HOLIDAYS · Matinee 2:00 and 3:45 · Evenings 7:00 and 8:45
SUNDAY	TUESDAY	THURSDAY	SATURDAY
1st William Farnum "The Heart of a Lion" "Nothing But Nerve" "Mutt and Jeff Cartoon"	**3rd** Mae Murray "FACE VALUE" "Bull's Eye" No. 11 SET OF DISHES	**5th** Robert Warwick "The False Friend" "Phoney Photos"	**7th** Gladys Brockwell "FOR LIBERTY" "Dismissal of Silver Phil"
8th Madge Evans "GATES OF GLADNESS" "Pink Pajamas" "Mutt and Jeff Cartoon"	**10th** Dorothy Phillips "BROADWAY LOVE" "Bull's Eye" No. 12	**12th** Alice Brady "The Divorce Game" "A Bird" Pig	**14th** Virginia Pearson "STOLEN HONOR" "The Coming of Faro Nell"
15th June Elvidge "Beautiful Mrs. Reynolds" "Hickory Hiram" "Mutt and Jeff Cartoon"	**17th** Franklyn Farnum "The Fighting Grin" "Bull's Eye" No. 13 SET OF DISHES	**19th** Clara Kimball Young "THE DARK SILENCE" "Who's Zoo"	**21st** Tom Mix "CUPID'S ROUND-UP" "The Widow Dangerous"
22nd Kitty Gordon "THE DIVINE SACRIFICE" "The Singing Keyhole" "Mutt and Jeff Cartoon"	**24th** Ruth Clifford "HANDS DOWN" "Bull's Eye" No. 14	**26th** Carlyle Blackwell "THE MARRIAGE MARKET" "Merry Mermaids"	**28th** Sonia Markova "A HEART'S REVENGE" "The Winning of the Mocking Bird"
29th Ethel Clayton "THE WHIMS OF SOCIETY" "It's a Cruel World" "Mutt and Jeff Cartoon"	WILLIAM FARNUM in "THE HEART OF A LION" Set of Dishes Given Away Tuesday, Sept. 3rd, and Tuesday, Sept. 17th Save Your Tickets Show Afternoon and Evening on LABOR DAY; Evening Only an ADMISSION DAY. See Below		
MONDAY, SEPT. 2—LABOR DAY CARLYLE BLACKWELL and EVELYN GREELEY "HIS ROYAL HIGHNESS" "Tucson Jennie's Heart"		MONDAY, Sept. 9—ADMISSION DAY JUNE ELVIDGE and ARTHUR ASHLEY "BROKEN TIES" "The Jests of Talky Jones"	

59

In this 1909 image from Val Tietz's album, the photographer was standing at the site where the library was until 2007. The middle structure (654 Chenery Street) was a hardware store. Only the building on the left remains and now houses a hair salon. In these photographs from the first few decades of the 20th century, downtown Glen Park looks like a still shot from a western. The next few decades would bring the neighborhood into the modern-day era. (Courtesy San Francisco Public Library.)

Four

THE BERNAL CUT AND SAN JOSE AVENUE

In 1928, just before the stock market crashed and sent the country spiraling into the Great Depression, the new San Jose Avenue opened for crosstown traffic. The highway certainly made Glen Park more accessible by automobile—the success of which was to change the whole face of San Francisco—but at the expense of demolishing whole streets and cutting off several pockets from downtown Glen Park. For part of its route, San Jose Avenue ran along what was called the Bernal Cut, the single track along which the San Francisco and San Jose Railroad had chugged since 1864. The systematic removal of the train tracks and widening of the cut was carefully documented by photographers. The resulting images are romantic—how astonishing to think of a real steam engine running along the border of Glen Park!—and convey the excitement of progress and innovation, as well as the satisfaction of hard work and solid results.

The San Francisco and San Jose Railroad (consolidated into the Southern Pacific, which was operated by the powerful Big Four) was running through Glen Park by 1964. The freight cars carried goods from factories in the South Bay to markets in downtown San Francisco, where a burgeoning population and economy created tremendous need. This train is a doubleheader, one engine pulling another. (Courtesy private collector.)

The tracks ran approximately 50 miles, from San Jose to San Francisco, and passed just southeast of Glen Park, running almost parallel to San Jose Avenue. After that, the line traversed the city south of Market Street, cutting through streets at uneven angles (even today, in the Mission District, one can find wedge-shaped lots because the train came through there) and coming to rest at the terminal at Howard and Eleventh Streets. (Courtesy private collector.)

This 1922 photograph, taken from the Miguel Street footbridge and looking northeast toward the Highland Avenue bridge (and downtown), shows the depth of the Bernal Cut ditch. The street on the left is Arlington. (Courtesy Dan Gustavson.)

Precita Creek initially created the opening later chosen for the Bernal Cut, but digging it deep enough for the railroad was still a major undertaking and the greatest barrier to finishing the line. (Courtesy private collector.)

This wonderful c. 1925 photograph, with a figure racing a freight train going north, looks south into Glen Park. The siding, or small portion of sidetrack, which breaks off to the right, used to permit a car to pull right alongside the back entrance of the Diamond Street Safeway store to deliver goods. The paths on the sides of the cut are unsophisticated water-runoff ditches. (Courtesy private collector.)

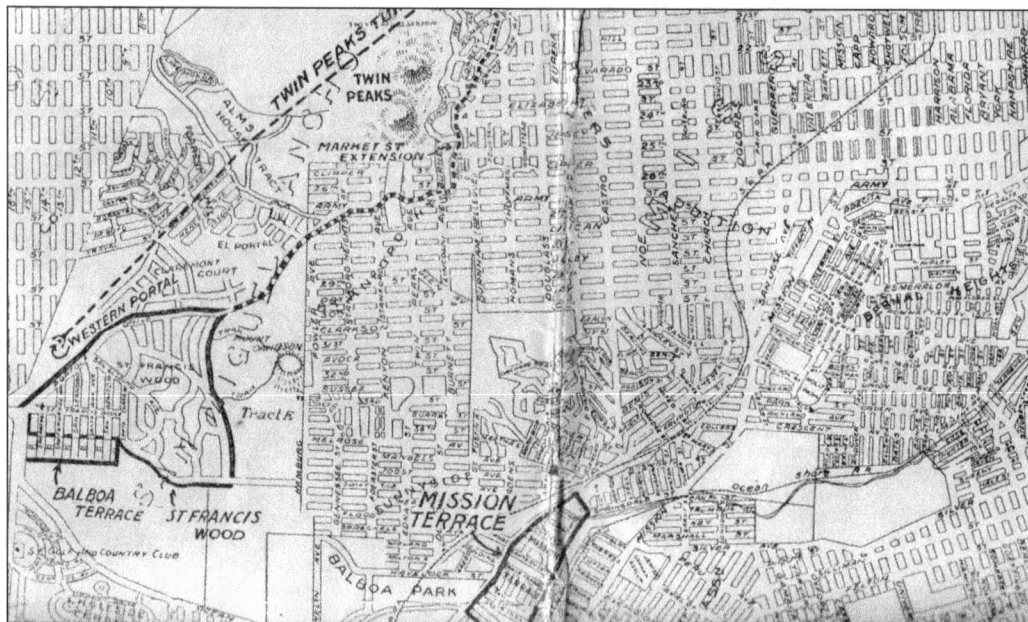

A c. 1906 Baldwin and Howell real estate map shows the train track winding its way along the Bernal Cut. It crossed Bosworth Street on a bridge, visible in the photograph on page 46. (Courtesy Richard Brandi.)

By the late 1920s, the Southern Pacific no longer needed the San Francisco and San Jose line, and the city began work to widen the ditch for a big boulevard. As this photograph testifies, the tracks were already gone by June 1929, and water pipes were being laid. The white building in the distance was the Ray Oil Burner Company at Rousseau Street and San Jose Avenue (right at the current northbound exit). (Courtesy private collector.)

This footbridge passed over the cut at Highland Avenue, and the neighborhood on the other side, College Hill, was often considered part of Glen Park, too. These men are probably digging the water main. (Courtesy private collector.)

This photograph, labeled "Bernal Cut Ground Breaking" and looking east along the tracks, is dated November 1929. The photographer was probably standing on the footbridge connecting Miguel Street and Richland Avenue. Arlington Street is on the left. Today there are pedestrian walkways on both sides of San Jose Avenue, and a community garden on the Arlington Street side. (Courtesy private collector.)

Just nine months later, the tracks are gone and the cut is significantly widened. The Miguel Street bridge is completed (the scaffolding would come down later) and the Highland Avenue one is in progress. Sewer and water pipes are going in (the former leading to the Glen Park water supply at the College Hill reservoir). Arlington Street is on the right. (Courtesy private collector.)

The author took this photograph from the Highland Avenue bridge, looking west toward the Miguel Street bridge, a similar vantage point as the previous photograph. Today the J Church runs down the center of San Jose Avenue. (Courtesy author.)

The railroad bridge over Bosworth Street was demolished and replaced by a new one—not for a train but for the six lanes of automobile traffic that would run along the new San Jose Avenue. In this view, looking down Bosworth Street away from central Glen Park, one can just make out the streetcar tracks that ran up until 1928 or 1929. (Courtesy Ken and Kathy Hoegger.)

Construction of the new bridge began in April 1929. The old Glen Park School (center) and Martha Hill (top right) help orient the viewer in this photograph, which looks west toward Diamond Street. (Courtesy private collector.)

Four months later, construction of the bridge was well under way. (Courtesy private collector.)

Today there are actually two bridges over Bosworth Street, this one for San Jose Avenue and another just east of this spot for the 280 Freeway, built in the 1950s. The bridge that motorists drive under today has been remodeled, probably when 280 went in. (Courtesy private collector.)

The new San Jose Avenue opened on April 16, 1930, two years after the work began. This photograph looks southwest at St. Mary's Avenue (the street underneath). Arlington Street is

on the right, and Merced Heights and City College are in the distance to the left. Monterey Boulevard is in the center. (Courtesy Dan Gustavson.)

The construction of San Jose Avenue (seen here from the Highland Avenue bridge looking east toward downtown San Francisco) capped off a period of frenzied building and growth in Glen Park. The years of the Great Depression and World War II were far leaner; little privately funded building took place during this time. By 1929, Glen Park was much more easily accessible from the east but still fairly isolated from the western parts of the city. That would change with the digging of O'Shaughnessy Boulevard. (Courtesy Dan Gustavson.)

Five

BOSWORTH, O'SHAUGHNESSY, 280, AND THE FREEWAY REVOLTS

When is enough enough? When is progress really a setback? The paving of O'Shaughnessy Boulevard was completed in 1940, connecting Glen Park with the western part of the city. Few people today would decry that advance. Just 15 years later, however, overzealous city planners decided that the two-lane road was not enough. Their new plan would have built a raised freeway along Bosworth Street and sent traffic tunneling under Twin Peaks to meet up with Lincoln Way near Golden Gate Park. A decade later, a similar but even more disruptive plan was unveiled. Residents claimed that with development being more or less finished in Glen Park, the area was already sufficiently serviced by the existing roads. Both times, local activists manage to shoot down the plans, saving over 100 houses and business from demolition and preserving some of the neighborhood's village-like character.

The 1950s were the era of the Freeway Revolts, a time when postwar enthusiasm for building and civic planning clashed with growing grassroots ideals. Many changes took place during the next few decades, each one taking away a little bit of the old Glen Park, but adding something of its own. The 280 Freeway went in as well as BART. Both necessitated taking out many home and streets, but both are also two of the reasons people find living in Glen Park so convenient today.

For the first four decades of the 20th century, O'Shaughnessy Boulevard (named after city engineer Michael O'Shaughnessy, responsible for Hetch Hetchy Dam and the West Portal Tunnel) did not exist, although rough goat paths may have wound up the hillside along the road's current location. This undated photograph, probably *c.* 1915, was taken where the boulevard begins today, looking east down Bosworth Street (also unpaved). The Dinky Line streetcars carried visitors from Mission Street to the Mission Park and Zoo entrance at Congo Street. These arches marked the entrance to the Crocker Estate.

In 1923, the streetcar tracks were gone, as was the zoo, which the Crocker Estate had built to attract potential home buyers. This car would have been coming down from Congo Street, which goes off to the left. Today Elk Street starts here, plunging steeply downhill toward the Recreation Center. The house on the right was demolished for the widening of Bosworth Street in the 1960s. (Courtesy private collector.)

Today the view looking down Bosworth Street is much changed, although the big wooden house, probably built between 1906 and 1910, still stands. It is fourth from the corner; only the (added on) garage and upper windows are visible here. (Courtesy author.)

This house may have been built as a summer and weekend home for wealthy San Franciscans from Nob Hill and Pacific Heights. The streets up behind it, namely Congo and Martha, are also included in Glen Park and were part of the original Crocker Estate housing tracts. The rest of the hill leading up to Mount Davidson was developed decades later. (Courtesy Sally Bland.)

This interesting 1930 photograph shows a paved but still not widened Bosworth Street between Hamerton and Burnside Avenues. Since the street ended at the canyon, there was very little car traffic on it. The Bosworth Street streetcar service ended in 1928 or 1929, but the single track was not taken out immediately. The houses on the left probably date from the 1920s. (Courtesy San Francisco Public Library.)

After the widening in 1964, Bosworth Street became a four-lane highway. The few buildings on the north side of the street were demolished. One of those (at Bosworth Street and Brompton Avenue) housed the public library, which then moved to 2909 Diamond Street. (Courtesy Richard Brandi.)

In the late 1930s, the city finally decided to build O'Shaughnessy Boulevard into the walls of Glen Canyon to link up with Bosworth Street and provide a direct automobile route from Glen Park to the western side of the city. In 1940, the project, which had already cost $1 million, ran out of funds and stalled temporarily. Here the road had been dug but not yet paved. (Courtesy private collector.)

Children play on the still-unfinished boulevard. The eastern side of Mount Davidson (Miraloma Park) was being developed around this time; however, goats still graze on the hillside and a small vegetable garden grows by the side of the road. (Courtesy private collector.)

Another wild and lonely shot of O'Shaughnessy Boulevard before it was completed shows two little white structures to the left, also visible in the photograph on the previous page. These houses no longer exist, and trees and vegetation have overtaken the roadsides. The houses above the boulevard are on Marietta Drive in Miraloma Park. (Courtesy private collector.)

The unique vantage point of this photograph captures the now-paved boulevard (completed in 1941), the upward rise of Mount Davidson, and the drop toward the canyon floor. Note the barns and houses on the Mount Davidson side and the road snaking steeply uphill. (Courtesy private collector.)

The drop from the boulevard to the canyon floor is steep and long. (Today the canyon is thick with tall nonnative eucalyptus, as well as Monterey pine and cypress, and one has little concept, driving along O'Shaughnessy Boulevard, of the precipitous drop.) The photographer was probably standing across the canyon, near the current location of Diamond Heights Boulevard. The houses at top are on El Sereno Court in Miraloma Park. (Courtesy San Francisco Public Library.)

Today a similar photograph (taken from Berkeley Way) shows how much the canyon has filled in with trees. (Courtesy author.)

The area where San Jose Avenue, Diamond Street, Monterey Boulevard, and 280 meet and cross is very confusing today, a maze of bridges and underpasses, as well as on-ramps and off-ramps. In 1917, the corner of San Jose Avenue and Diamond Street was still a sleepy country crossroads, although the streetcar did run past here. (Courtesy Ken Hoegger.)

In 1923, all of Diamond Street between Bosworth Street and San Jose Avenue was built with homes and small businesses. The photographer was standing on the side of the road, looking north toward downtown Glen Park, as a team of workers installed water pipelines. Today these houses are all gone, and the BART station stands in their place. (Courtesy San Francisco Public Library.)

In 1942, an outbound streetcar turns from Diamond Street onto Monterey Boulevard, heading west. The 1930s–era houses in the background on San Jose Avenue were demolished just two decades after their construction to make way for the new freeway. (Courtesy Jack Tillmany.)

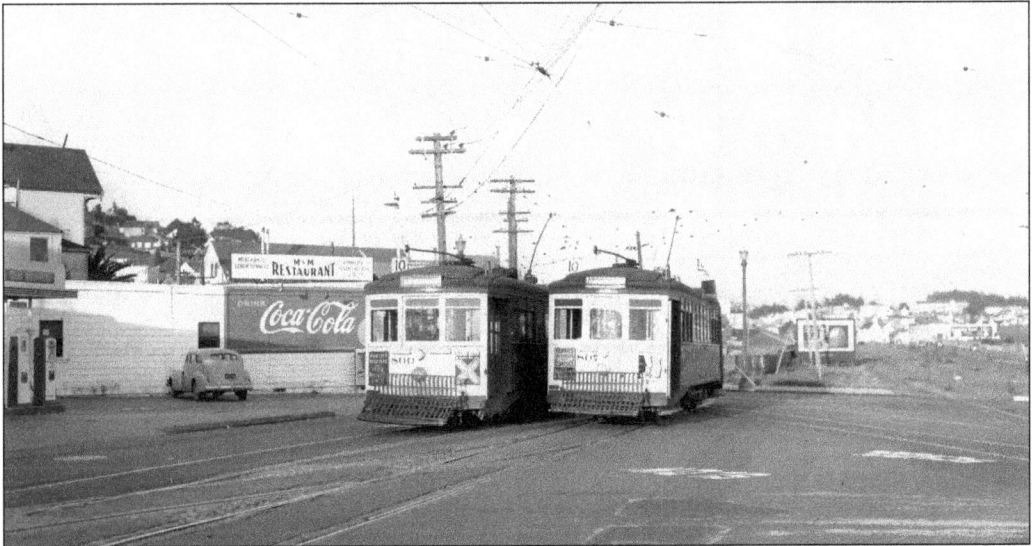

Two No. 10 streetcars pass each other going opposite ways at Monterey and San Jose. Here the photographer was looking northeast, with the houses of Glen Park at left and Bernal Heights at right. The white building on the far right may be the Ray Oil Burner Company, at Bosworth Street and Rousseau, now replaced with modern homes. A decade later, great changes were to come to this busy intersection, making it far less pedestrian-friendly and cutting a neighborhood in half. (Courtesy Jack Tillmany.)

TRANSPORTATION SECTION OF THE MASTER PLAN OF SAN FRANCISCO

TRAFFICWAYS PLAN

——————— FREEWAY

——————— MAJOR THOROUGHFARE

— — — — — SECONDARY THOROUGHFARE

= = = = = = EXPRESSWAY TREATMENT

::::::::::::::::: PARKWAY TREATMENT

THIS PLAN WAS ADOPTED BY RESO-
LUTION NUMBER 3948 ON JULY 17,
1951, AND AMENDED BY RESOLUTION
NUMBER 4423 OF THE CITY PLANNING
COMMISSION AT A REGULAR MEETING
HELD ON MAY 19, 1955.

The heyday of freeway building, and the nationwide Freeway Revolts that followed, took place in the late 1950s and 1960s. After the deprivations of the Great Depression and the war years, city planners were eager to build and improve, sometimes misguidedly. Interstate 280 was completed in 1957. Three years later, the Highway Department unveiled this map in the *San Francisco Chronicle*, displaying a network of additional proposed freeways, some eventually built, some not. Plans such as these were sprouting up in cities across America, including Boston, Milwaukee, Portland, Seattle, Baltimore, and Washington, D.C. (Courtesy Richard Brandi.)

Hermini Baxter, 64, a lifelong resident of Glen Park and the daughter of Augustus Straub, the saloon owner, was one of many locals who expressed instant concern upon the publication of the Trafficways Map. The Crosstown Freeway was to begin at 280, run alongside Bosworth Street and part of O'Shaughnessy Boulevard, then shoot through Glen Canyon, tunnel under Portola Drive and Twin Peaks, and emerge to join up with the Western Freeway (also never built) near Seventh Avenue. It would have destroyed 120 homes and 13 businesses in Glen Park. (Courtesy San Francisco Public Library.)

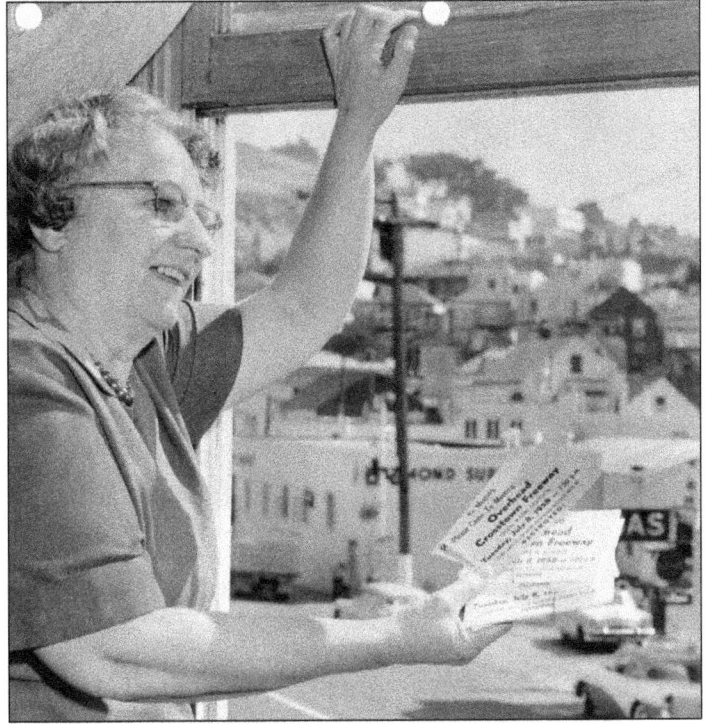

Please Come To Meeting
Overhead
Crosstown Freeway
GLEN PARK SCHOOL
Tuesday, July 8, 1958 -- 7:30 p.m.
COME AND LEARN HOW GLEN PARK DISTRICT WILL BE
DESTROYED

Hermini Baxter organized meetings and passed out hundreds of flyers, finally succeeding in stopping the construction of the freeway. An article in a newspaper from June 20, 1958, quotes a city official defending the plan: "Someone is always hurt by construction of a freeway. It comes back to the basic question confronting the city: Does San Francisco want freeways, or not?" For Glen Parkers, the answer was a resounding "no." Today enthusiasm for urban freeways has dimmed, leading to smarter planning and the tearing down of many 1960s–era behemoths.

83

Although the Crosstown Freeway was stopped, the neighborhood had already been disrupted by the construction of Interstate 280 in 1957. In 1950, a group of girls stops to pose during a birthday party behind the Conte family house at Lamartine and Calvert Streets. A portion of Lamartine Street remains, but this block was seized by eminent domain and torn down. Ann Marie is at center, holding her baby sister Kathy. (Courtesy Kathy Hoegger.)

The Conte house on Lamartine was only about 10 years old when it was demolished in the late 1950s. Before the construction of 280, Danton, Lamartine, Badger, and Goerum Streets ran right through to Glen Park; residents could walk there in minutes to shop and catch the streetcar or bus. Today the streets are totally isolated and dead end at the 280 retaining wall. From left to right are Frank, Yolanda, Kathy, Josephine, and Ann Marie Conte and grandfather Giuseppe Rinaldi. (Courtesy Kathy Hoegger.)

In 1953, just four years before 280 went in, homes lined San Jose Avenue (viewed here from Monterey Boulevard; Diamond Street goes off to the left). Crossing guards stand at the corner (Glen Park School is just a block away) and parents walk their children across the street. Today this is the on-ramp to San Jose Avenue and 280 North. (Courtesy Dan Gustavson.)

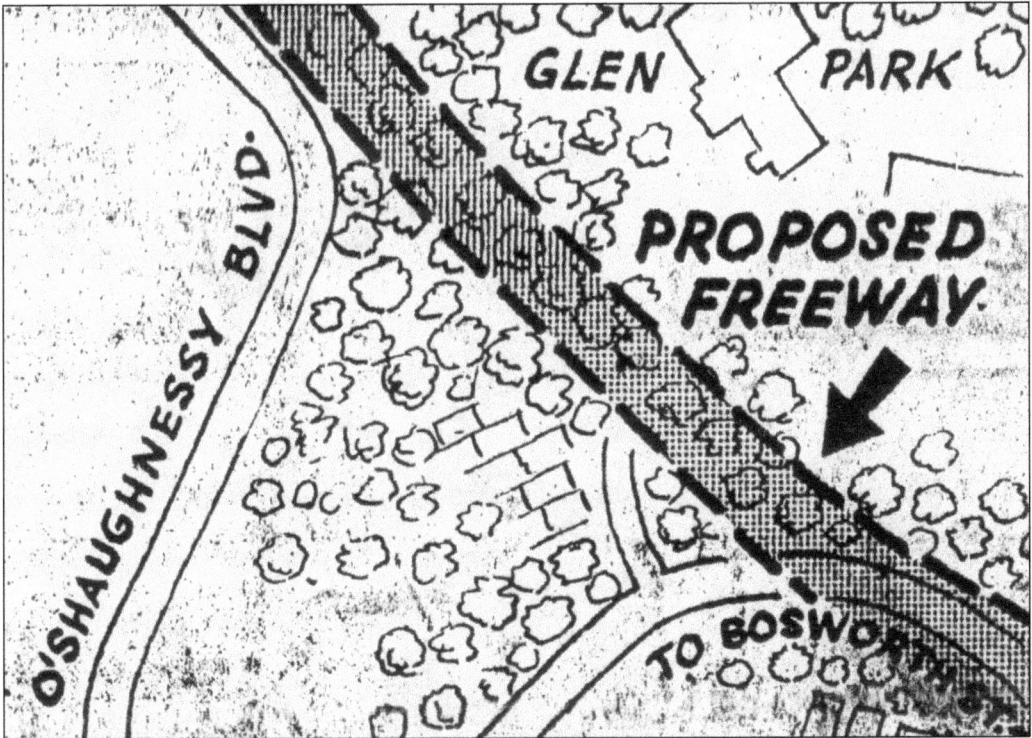

In 1967, residents once again had to step forward to protect the integrity of their neighborhood. The city wanted to build a four-lane highway cutting across the ball field, offering motorists a straight shot from Bosworth Street up to Portola. A trio of women who came to be known as the Gum Tree Girls (Zoanne Nordstrom, Joan Seiwald, and Jerry Arkush) lobbied to get the plan thrown out—and succeeded.

O'Shaughnessy Boulevard was one of the most positive of the great transportation-related changes that were wrought upon Glen Park in the 1940s, 1950s, and 1960s. In 1950, the roadside was still barren; the eucalyptus would grow to astonishing heights in the next 50 years. This photograph was taken by a child playing in the open fields off Stillings Avenue in Miraloma Park. (Courtesy Valerie Chester Hoover.)

Six

THE FAIRMOUNT TRACT

The triangle formed by Castro Street, Thirtieth Street, and San Jose Avenue is commonly known as Fairmount, Fairmount Heights, or the Fairmount Tract. Although Thirtieth Street is the official divider between Noe Valley and Glen Park, the Fairmount Tract is often referred to as Upper Noe, and residents on the northern end frequently head to Twenty-fourth Street rather than Chenery Street for their shopping. Development in the Fairmount area began in the 1860s, much earlier than in the western part (the "heart") of Glen Park. As was the case in Noe Valley, most settlers were Irish and decidedly working class. As Mae Silver explains in her definitive book, *Rancho San Miguel* (1992), the residents of Noe Valley, Eureka Valley, and the Fairmount Tract were the blue-collar workers who "cleaned, built, repaired and supported the folks in the 'fancy' neighborhoods in town. They supplied the workforce behind the wheel that drove downtown San Francisco." Fairmounters were not only maids and housekeepers, but also streetcar drivers, policemen, firefighters, and later teachers, lawyers, and doctors.

Today the Fairmount Tract is a lovely neighborhood of restored Victorian homes. Chenery Street is the main drag (and used to have multiple corner stores), but side streets like Randall, Miguel, and Fairmount Streets provide scenic charm. A walk down unparalleled Laidley Street might lead one to posit that this area is a district unto itself, with a unique character not found anywhere else in the city.

The Fairmount Tract was developed beginning in the 1860s. Some dwellings were individual homes—farmhouses built by their owners. Others were part of mini housing developments, or several houses put up at the same time by a realtor or contractor. These identical houses on the 300 block of Arlington Street, between Mateo and Miguel Streets, were probably such a group. In the background are the hills of the Excelsior District. (Courtesy private collector.)

In 1912, Allie Johnson, a third-generation Glen Parker, stands on the corner of Chenery and Fairmount Streets in front of a house her grandfather helped build. It was not uncommon for families to put down deep roots in one neighborhood, to have many children there, and for those children to marry and raise their own families on the same street. Members of Johnson's extended family lived all up and down the first few blocks of Chenery Street and are an indelible part of its history. (Courtesy Cathie Schafer.)

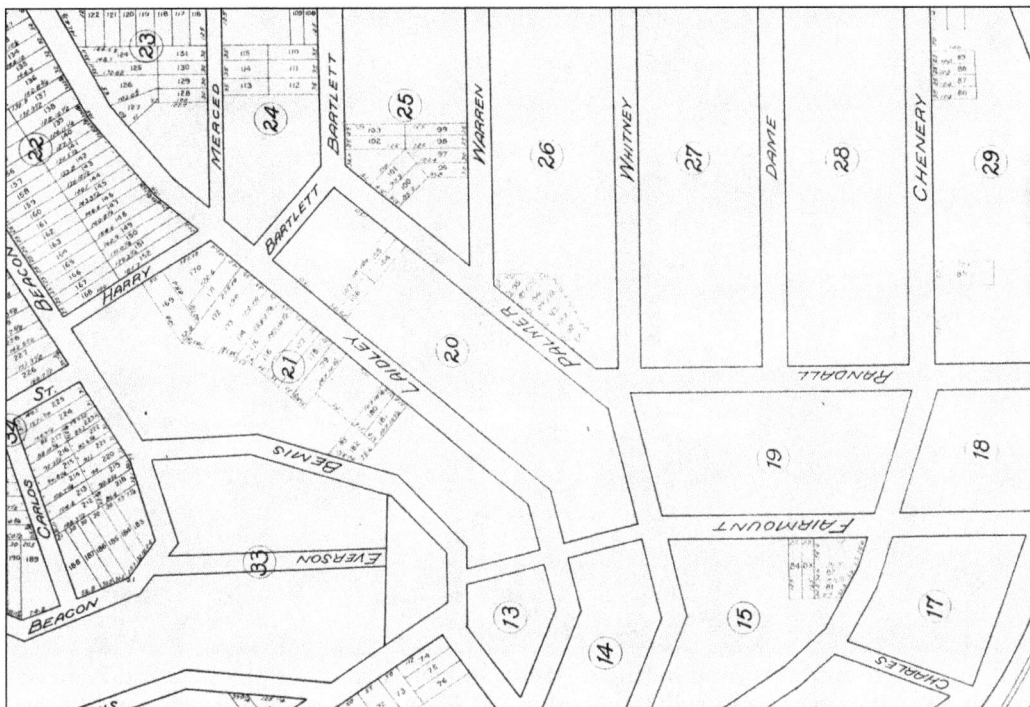

Very few lots were marked out on this 1871 map, suggesting that most homes in the Fairmount Tract date from later than that. One of the most powerful early landowners in the area was James Laidley, a wealthy North Beach entrepreneur who was also on the board of the San Francisco and San Jose Railroad, which passed nearby. Laidley, who passed away in 1876, came from Philadelphia; some think that he named the district after his hometown's Fairmount Park. Another possible namesake is Comstock Lode millionaire James Graham Fair, after whom the Fairmont Hotel was also named. (Courtesy Jane Radcliffe.)

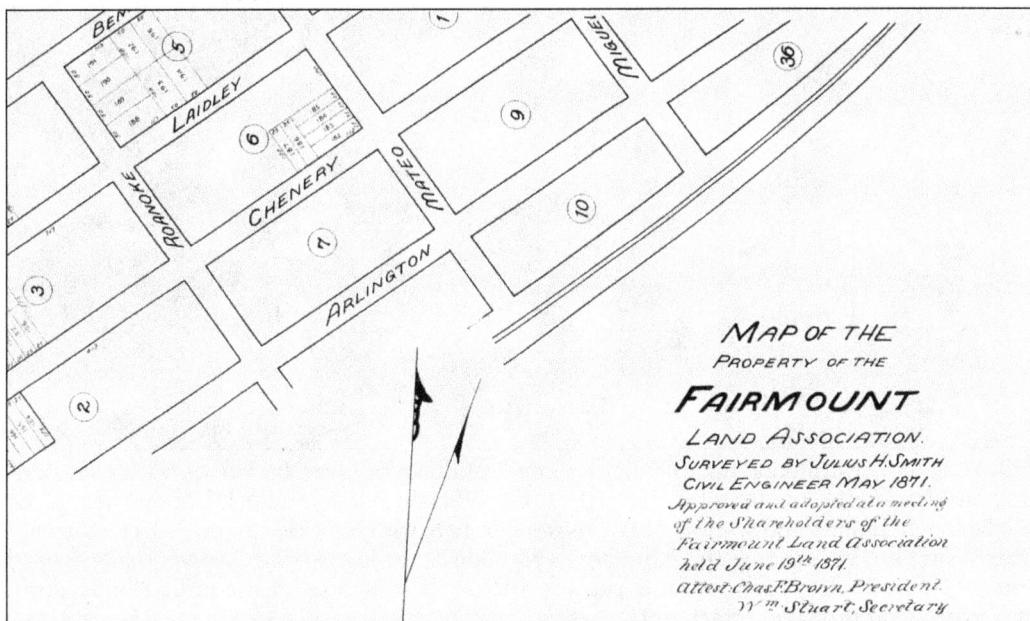

William J. Sullivan was born in Ireland in 1846. His name appears on the 1880 San Francisco census, about the same year he built this house at 220 Arlington Street, the first one on the street. The Sullivans later built several more houses on the block, and as their nine children grew up and moved into their own homes right nearby, Arlington Street became known as Sullivan Alley. It was one of William's sons, James J., who owned the barn pictured in the photograph on page 24. (Courtesy Michael Waldstein.)

Like most early Fairmount and Glen Park settlers, William Sullivan (at left with his eight sons and one daughter) came from humble origins. His official trade was a dock laborer (he ran the public weigh station), and several of his sons worked there with him. He also owned a lumberyard across San Jose Avenue from the Arlington Street house; the lumberyard was eventually divided into 10 lots and sold. Here the family poses in 1921 at their vacation house in La Honda, down the coast. (Courtesy Joan Strachan.)

In 1927, Frances Sullivan, one of William's granddaughters, plays in front of the 220 Arlington Street house with neighbor Katie O'Leary and her sister. Two doors down, on the corner of Arlington and Charles Streets, stands a brown shingled house that was originally the Sullivan family barn. It was converted to a house in 1924 and was sold or given to the oldest Sullivan son. (Courtesy Joan Strachan.)

This real estate tax receipt from 1883 covered two of William Sullivan's buildings—lots 12 and 13, probably the house at 220 Arlington Street, and the barn next door. (In 1933, William's son Thomas built a house in between the other two, at 214.) (Courtesy David and Lea Schermerhorn.)

If the Sullivans were the kings of Arlington Street, the McLaughlin-Johnsons were equally influential a block away, on Chenery Street. John L. McLaughlin (believed to be the man with the horse standing in front of three of the houses he helped build at Chenery and Fairmount Streets) was born in Ireland in 1833 and immigrated to the United States in 1835. He grew up in Boston and headed west with his wife, Elizabeth, in 1865. They came to San Francisco via the Panama Canal and settled in the Chenery Street area. John was a carpenter and worked on many of the houses along Chenery Street; he was also one of the men instrumental in building the volunteer firehouse on Diamond Street. (Courtesy Cathie Schafer.)

John and Elizabeth had eight children; the oldest daughter was Mary, who married Albert Johnson. Albert and Mary lived and raised their 11 children in many of the homes in the 100–200 block of Chenery Street. They ran a grocery at 200 Chenery Street and a saloon/liquor store out of five different locations, including Nos. 111, 113, and 241 Chenery Street (one is visible in the photograph on page 55). Here they pose around 1900 in the backyard of one of their homes. (Courtesy Cathie Schafer.)

Around 1915, one of John and Elizabeth's daughters, Loretta Johnson (in white), along with two cousins and a friend, smile for the photographer in the backyard of one of the Chenery Street houses. Looking east, beyond was nothing but farms and open space right up to San Jose Avenue. (Arlington Street runs parallel to Chenery Street for several blocks but ends at Randall Street.) (Courtesy Cathie Schafer.)

The three houses on the right were most likely built by John L. McLaughlin. The one on the corner is 163 Chenery Street, somewhat altered from its original state. The third house from the corner, 153–155 Chenery Street, was jacked up in 1923 to add a garage, which accounts for its irregular height. (Courtesy author.)

In the last few decades, Laidley Street has become the place to be in the Fairmount Tract, but it was not always that way. Elevation wise, Laidley towers above Chenery and Arlington Streets. Today the sweeping views are prized, but in the days before cars, living on a hill meant hiking to get anywhere, and often it was the poorer folks who had to settle up high. For this 1927 shot, the photographer was standing on Thirtieth Street looking up at the beginning of Laidley Street. (Courtesy Larry Wisch.)

Today Laidley Street is divided for the one block between Thirtieth Street and Noe. After the 1906 earthquake, some people fled the destroyed downtown area for the Fairmount Tract, which was considered far enough away to be "safe," but still close to the shops and transportation of Noe Valley. Children on Laidley Street and nearby went to Kate Kennedy Grammar School, now a child development center, on Thirtieth and Noe Streets. (Courtesy author.)

On the corner of Laidley and Fairmount Streets sits the Halloween-perfect Poole-Bell mansion, built in 1890. Neighborhood rumors have it that an African American woman named Mary Ellen Pleasant once ran a madam business out of the house. Pleasant was a notorious character in San Francisco history. Born into slavery in Georgia around 1815, Pleasant became the business partner of wealthy San Francisco businessman Thomas Bell in the 1880s, and lived with him and his wife, Theresa. Pleasant's story is steeped in lore and apocrypha—some called her the mother of civil rights in California; others labeled her the "wickedest woman in San Francisco" and whispered about black magic. But Pleasant never lived in the Poole-Bell mansion, though Theresa Bell did move into it in 1906, two years after Pleasant's death. (Courtesy author.)

Most of the cottages and small homes on the north side of Laidley have been added on to—generally very gracefully—and give little clue to their modest beginnings. After several apartment buildings went up in the 1950s, neighbors protested and had the area downzoned to R-1—single-family homes only. (Courtesy Larry Wisch.)

Beginning in the 1980s, architect Jeremy Kotas was involved with redesigning at least six houses on the block, including number 140 (pictured here), called the Eyebrow or Owl House. Kotas's designs are dramatic, imaginative, and tasteful. Others followed suit on their own, and some would say that Kotas was responsible for the metamorphosis of an entire street, quite a feat. The Pooles (builders of the Poole-Bell mansion) originally owned this property and used it as their gardens. (Courtesy Dick Ingraham.)

The green house at 104 Laidley Street is referred to as a "dingbat"—a building added on to at random over the years, resulting in an often inviting mélange of styles. Its current owner has done much to pull the house together, and today it stands out as one of the most interesting homes on the block. The blue house next door is another colorful Kotas creation. (Courtesy Larry Wisch.)

A 1927 photograph shows the paved portion of Laidley Street ending at Noe Street, just a block from Thirtieth Street, and a number of vacant lots. Today trees grow all over the hillside beyond. (Courtesy Larry Wisch.)

Two children roller skate down Laidley Street in the 1940s. (Courtesy Daniel Oppenheim.)

Right in between 98 and 100 Laidley Street, Harry Street begins its 236-step ascension to Beacon Street. As captivating as the Filbert Steps of Telegraph Hill but far less traveled, the mostly wooden Harry Stairs are home to a handful of storybook cottages and a few almost-estates with large, terraced grounds. The cottages at 28 and 30 Harry Street were the first houses on the block, built in 1904 and 1905 by the Foster family, who ran back and forth between them. The stairway is pictured here completely open, but today it is lush with trees and vines. (Courtesy Daniel Oppenheim.)

For some time, the stairs went only as far as the Fosters' two homes. In the 1920s, they were extended almost all the way up to Beacon Street and were completed in the early 1990s. In this photograph, the Fosters pose on the landing outside the front door of 30 Harry Street, looking south. Laidley Street is downhill to the left. (Courtesy Daniel Oppenheim.)

Seven

A REAL NEIGHBORHOOD
SCHOOLS, PARKS, AND CHURCHES

By 1910, Glen Park had a fast-growing population, and the new residents' children needed a school. The current Glen Park School's main entrance is at 151 Lippard Avenue, but anyone driving down Bosworth Street cannot help but notice the imposing blue structure, erected in 1935 by the Works Progress Administration, with its pedestrian footbridge leading over the street to Glen Park proper. Records show that the first school was built in 1910 or 1912, although a photograph of a class with a boy holding a "Glen Park Grammar School 1909" placard leads one to surmise that classes were held for at least one year in a temporary building. But children need to play as well as learn, and in 1922, the city acquired Glen Park Canyon from the Crocker Estate and built the clubhouse (another WPA project) there in 1938. The first generation of children began to play baseball on the flat field where 50 years before, Alfred Clarke had dammed Islais Creek to power his waterworks, and cows and goats had descended from the hills of Glen Canyon to drink. With schools and parks, baseball for the kids, and tennis for the parents, Glen Park was no longer an Outside Land. It was a good place to live.

The old Glen Park School (built in 1910) is visible in the distance of this 1927 view looking southwest down Chenery Street at Natick Street. In 1935, the school was replaced with the current building. (Courtesy Dan Gustavson.)

Not a child dared to smile in this 1916 first-grade class photograph. Glen Park School went from kindergarten through eighth grade; after that, students went to Balboa High. (Courtesy San Francisco Public Library.)

Florence Lucassen, who lived with her parents and seven siblings on Diamond Street, is the only girl on the bottom row. In 1928, she was in the seventh or eighth grade. (Courtesy Valerie Chester Hoover.)

The Glen Park baseball team poses on the school yard in the 1920s or 1930s. Fairmount Hill rises in the background to the right, and Gold Mine to the left. (Courtesy private collector.)

The Fairmount School, at Randall and Chenery Streets, existed long before its Glen Park counterpart; records show 137 registered pupils in 1870. The original school had a wood-burning stove and a planked school yard. Ruth Johnson, the little girl on the right holding the teddy bear, was probably a first grader in this 1911 photograph. She grew up on Chenery Street. (Courtesy Cathie Schafer.)

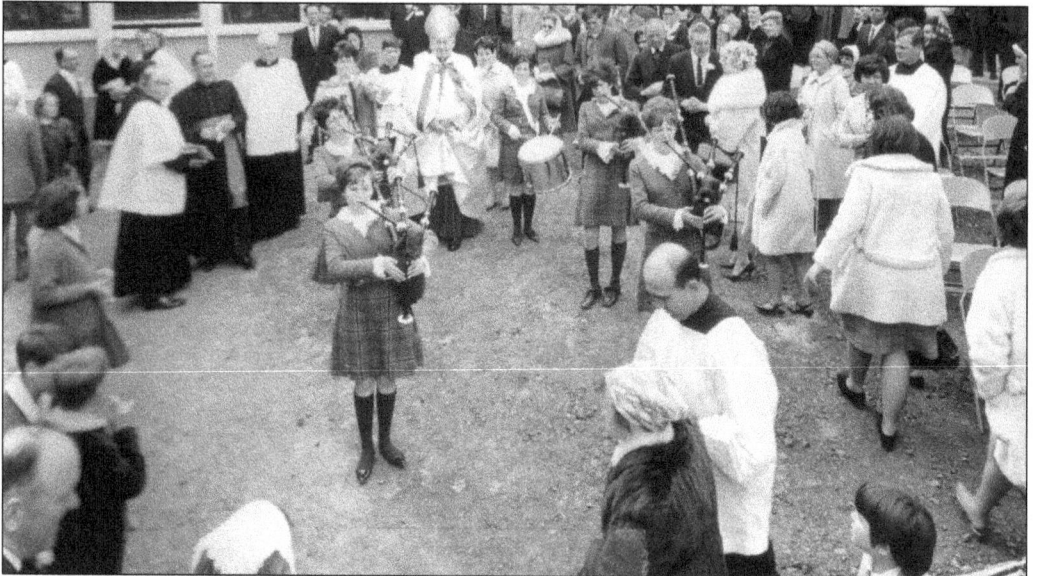

In 1966, the St. John's Catholic elementary school moved from its location adjacent to the parish church, on St. Mary's Avenue near Mission Street, to 925 Chenery Street at Burnside Avenue, near the canyon. This is a photograph from the dedication ceremony, when St. John's was called John F. Kennedy Memorial School. (Courtesy St. John's School.)

Evelyn Lucassen and friends dressed up for graduation day in 1929, with the hills of Glen Park in the distance. Evelyn is wearing glasses and a fur stole over her middy blouse. (Courtesy Valerie Hoover.)

Ann Marie Conte (second from left) was a kindergartner at Glen Park School in 1945. Ann Marie and her sister lived on Lamartine Street across San Jose Avenue from Glen Park, and they were able to walk to school. (Today the route would be more circuitous because of the freeway.) In the 1950s, Glen Park School changed from K-8 to K-6. (Courtesy Kathy Hoegger.)

Until 1922, the Crocker Estate owned the Glen Park Canyon fields, which were used mainly as picnic grounds. Clubs and groups would rent the space and hold lively parties. Eventually neighbors began to wish for a safe, public place for their children to play and urged the city to acquire the land. It bought all 101 acres of the canyon in 1922 for $20,000. In 1937, the WPA started work on the clubhouse that exists to this day. (Courtesy private collector.)

A 1942 photograph taken from Martha Hill provides a broad panorama of the area before trees and further development completely obscured the views. O'Shaughnessy Boulevard was brand new, just one year old; Bosworth Street had yet to be widened; and the two houses that straddle Elk Street here were demolished in the 1960s (the photographs on page 74 show older views of the intersection). Today Diamond Heights Boulevard picks up where Elk Street ends, hugging the outside of the hill and giving drivers a stunning view of the canyon. Twin Peaks is in the distance. (Courtesy private collector.)

In 1952, John Bagatelos, at top right next to the coach, played for the Glen Park Recreation Center baseball team. Bagatelos grew up at 732 Chenery Street with his parents, who had emigrated from Greece. (Courtesy Karen Bagatelos.)

Ed Dunn (at bat) grew up in Glen Park, was a prisoner of war in Germany during World War II, became a San Francisco firefighter, and founded one of the city's recycling centers. He passed away in 2006. (Courtesy private collector.)

After their purchase by the city in 1922, the canyon and park quickly became a haven for neighborhood kids. In 1928, Genevieve Lucassen stands in a eucalyptus tree in the Glen Park playground. Genevieve was one of the eight Lucassen children who grew up in the small house at 2660 Diamond Street. She would have been about 18 here. (Courtesy Valerie Chester Hoover.)

Genevieve's daughter Valerie Chester (left) and her cousin Melvyn Johnson ride bikes in the playground in 1940. Elk Street is directly behind them, and Chenery Street begins at right. (Courtesy Valerie Chester Hoover.)

Rose Fagnani, born in Mendocino County in 1907, moved to Surrey Street with her husband in the 1930s. In 1938, they bought one of the identical brand-new houses on Chenery Street near Elk Street and raised their two daughters there. Rose (first row, second from right) played tennis competitively with the Glen Park club through the 1940s and 1950s. She turns 100 this year and still lives on Chenery Street. (Courtesy Rose Fagnani.)

Silver Tree Day Camp began in 1961 with the intention of providing a summertime outdoor experience for city children. (The Glenridge Cooperative Nursery School uses the Silver Tree facilities during the school year.) Originally, busses picked up and dropped off the campers, but in the 1980s, the bus system was dropped, leading to a controversy involving parents driving into the park and creating congestion and noise pollution. Cars were banned from the park in the late 1990s, and peace returned to the canyon. Since 1997, the annual Glen Park Festival has helped raise funds to send San Francisco kids to Silver Tree. (Courtesy private collector.)

Glen Canyon is not the only green area in the vicinity. Dorothy Erskine Park, atop Martha Hill, from whose vantage point so many of Glen Park's panoramas were taken, was dedicated in 1979. Mayor Dianne Feinstein (far left) attended the dedication, along with, from left to right, Mary Burns, Tom Malloy (former director of Parks and Recreation), Dorothy Erskine (founder of the Greenbelt Alliance), and neighbor Ken Hoegger. (Courtesy Ken and Kathy Hoegger.)

For the children of Glen Park and Diamond Heights, there is almost no greater place to be than Walter Haas Playground, a four-acre park located on the northeast corner of Diamond Heights Boulevard and Addison Street. The almost $2 million remodeling was completed in November 2005 and boasts a dog run, walking path, basketball courts, and some of the best views in the city. (Courtesy author.)

Since the 1960s, there have been three churches in Diamond Heights, but before that, there was just the Catholic parish church, St. John the Evangelist, at 19 St. Mary's Avenue right near Mission Street. (Its rectory fronts Bosworth Street.) The parish also includes Sunnyside, Holly Park, and Diamond Heights, and St. John's School was adjacent to the church before moving to Chenery Street in 1967. The photograph below shows the first communion class of 1905. Built in 1903, St. John's was a refuge for people fleeing the fire-damaged parts of the city after the earthquake. Historian Dolan Eargle wrote in the *Glen Park News*, "Church archives record accounts of thousands in carts, wagons, on horseback, or simply trudging along Mission Road laden with baggage." From the beginning, Glen Park has always welcomed those in need. (Both courtesy St. John the Evangelist.)

Eight

DIAMOND HEIGHTS

Before Diamond Heights was Diamond Heights (a name invented by the San Francisco Redevelopment Agency), it was referred to by the three hills it comprises: Red Rock, Gold Mine, and Fairmount. Cows grazed there, families picnicked, and people ran their dogs. There were few trees; it was a wild and windswept place, commanding wide-open views in every direction. Only scattered farmhouses, generally Swiss or German families, existed on the peaks. There were certainly no luxury homes. And yet, it was not a "blighted area," as the San Francisco Redevelopment Agency claimed in 1953 when they chose the three hills as the site of a new housing project. That term bothered residents and neighbors, who were not happy with the prospect of having their homes seized or seeing modern construction take over the open spaces. However, housing was in short supply in San Francisco, and these 325 acres were one of the few large undeveloped areas. The agency promised an enlightened, tasteful plan, which would use natural contours as guidelines and work with, not against, the topography. Today Diamond Heights is a sort of small town unto itself, with a shopping center surrounded by attractive housing of varying size and style, catering to all income levels. If one asks a Diamond Heights homeowner why they think their neighborhood is the best in the city, they will talk about the harmonious combination of the peaceful suburban ambiance with incredible views and a central San Francisco location.

In the 1950s, from the lower slopes of Bernal Heights, above Mission Street, the three hills of Diamond Heights stand out clearly. From left to right they are Fairmount, Gold Mine, and Red Rock (Mount Davidson, topped with trees and its white cross, is beyond). Gold Mine and Red Rock both rise to approximately 680 feet above sea level, and Fairmount to 550. (Courtesy San Francisco Redevelopment Agency.)

Like Twin Peaks to the north, mid-century Diamond Heights was still rustic and rural, with humble wooden farmhouses, horses, cows, and goats. (Courtesy San Francisco Redevelopment Agency.)

In 1961, the tops of the three hills (from top to bottom are Fairmount, Gold Mine, and Red Rock) were leveled to make way for the new housing development called Diamond Heights. Portola is in the foreground, with Clipper snaking off to the left. Glen Canyon runs alongside Diamond Heights to the right. Note the newly completed clubhouse for Silver Tree Day Camp. (Courtesy San Francisco Redevelopment Agency.)

Construction has begun in this photograph of Red Rock and Gold Mine (Fairmount is just cut off at the top). The shopping center is in place, as is the elementary school just below. The school was later declared seismically unfit and today houses a police department training facility. A public library was also planned, but it was never built because of the lack of funds. Many of the streets on Red Rock and Gold Mine are named after precious stones: Amethyst, Quartz, Turquoise, Amber, Cameo, Topaz, Jade, and Ora. Fairmount Hill is home to the Glen Park Fire Station and Walter Haas Playground. (Courtesy San Francisco Redevelopment Agency.)

Buck Tergis grew up at 245 Beacon Street. (Today he lives just below on Laidley Street.) Here he stands in 1951 with his parents and younger brother in the backyard of the Beacon Street house, built by his mother, Sara Benezra, in 1932. She liked the location because she could run her goats in the open space all around. Sara had grown up on her grandmother's farm at 2010 Castro Street. When Diamond Heights was being planned in the 1950s, Sara fought to keep her Beacon Street house from being demolished, and she was successful. (Courtesy Turk Tergis.)

A 1927 overview of Fairmount Hill clearly shows Sara Benezra's house, a solitary square on Beacon Street, the unpaved road that runs across the top right corner of this photograph. Laidley Street is parallel to Beacon Street to the northeast; the huge rocky mass on top was the Gray Brothers Quarry; and the sharp white turn on the bottom left is Diamond Street. The open space in the middle (Fairmount Hill) is now built up with Digby, Everson, Addison, Farnum, and Moreland Streets. (Courtesy Buck Tergis.)

Seen from behind, this small farm on Red Rock Hill was built by William A. Tracy in the late 1800s or early 1900s. Its address was on Twenty-eighth Street, the dirt road that runs in front of it, but today the house would sit near Amber Street and the old elementary school. Tracy died in 1942, and his daughter later sold the property to the Sweisgood family, who ran a farm in between Duncan and Clipper Streets. George Sweisgood sold all his land to the Redevelopment Agency in the 1950s. (Courtesy Bill Tracy.)

William Tracy raised his two children in this house, and his grandson, Bill Tracy, remembers playing there as a child. Bill remained in Glen Park and owned The Lodge, a bar at the corner of Diamond and Wilder Streets, for 27 years, until 2002. (Courtesy Bill Tracy.)

This 1947 view looks south from lower Twin Peaks over Red Rock Hill, with its scattered farmhouses. The horizontal street in the foreground is Portola. The arrows were meant to indicate the project about to be completed, the extension of Clipper Street from below, in Noe Valley, all the way up the hill to link with Portola. George Sweisgood, owner of the farmhouse at Clipper and Duncan Streets, center, fought hard to keep his land but failed. (Courtesy Richard Brandi.)

About 13 years later, the redevelopment of Diamond Heights had begun. This photograph is taken from near the top of Twin Peaks. (Courtesy San Francisco Redevelopment Agency.)

Gold Mine Hill is still untouched in this view from Bosworth Street looking north along Elk Street, with the baseball field to the left. In the 1800s, city planners had subdivided, on paper, the whole Diamond Heights area in an impossible grid pattern that was never implemented. Then, in 1905, the famed urban planner Daniel Burnham was brought to San Francisco to devise a comprehensive beautification program. He drew up an innovative plan for Diamond Heights that included contoured streets encircling (not crossing) the hills. Burnham's topography-savvy ideas may owe something to the fact that his home base was not in the financial district or Nob Hill, but at his "Eagle's Nest" atop Twin Peaks, affording him a unique perspective. The earthquake hit just days after Burnham handed in his report, and most of his ideas never came to be. Fifty years later, developers picked up where Burnham had left off. (Courtesy San Francisco Redevelopment Agency.)

Before the redevelopment, the population of Diamond Heights was about 375. After, it grew to 7,300, with about 15 percent of the 325 acres in use. This wooden farmhouse (possibly a Sears mail-order house) survived the transition, and it still exists at 70 Gold Mine Drive, across from the shopping center. (Courtesy San Francisco Redevelopment Agency.)

Before the makeover, Diamond Heights was pure country and largely poor. Most of the inhabitants were small-time farmers or folks who simply enjoyed living a quiet, solitary life. (Courtesy San Francisco Redevelopment Agency.)

This radio station (the structure with the letters on the side) was located in the wilds of the hills. (Courtesy San Francisco Redevelopment Agency.)

A hike up Mount Davidson, to the west, affords probably the very best view of Diamond Heights. Here one can see Gold Mine Hill and the same radio station. The houses in the foreground are part of Miraloma Park. (Courtesy San Francisco Redevelopment Agency.)

In 1920, as now, Thirtieth Street, running west, ends at the foot of Gold Mine Hill. On the left is the old Gray Brothers Quarry, which was shut down before 1920; the hole it left behind was filled in by the city in the 1950s. For years before its demise, neighbors, incensed by the quarry's constant dust and debris, were lobbying to have it shut down. An unhappy former quarry employee walked up to George Gray and shot him dead. That employee, Joseph LoCoco, was tried but never convicted. (Courtesy Bill Yenne.)

From the same vantage point today, atop Billy Goat Hill, one can still pick out the four-sided peaked roof to the right. Straight ahead, where just a few isolated houses existed before, run Beacon Street, Diamond Heights Boulevard, Topaz Way, and Ora Way, in ascending order. Billy Goat Hill was preserved and is now a city park; it is accessible from above by Beacon Street. (Courtesy author.)

Valerie Chester Hoover grew up on Stillings Avenue on the Miraloma Park-Glen Park border and played daily with the neighborhood kids in the open space where Mercato Court and Malta Drive are today. Their scenic backdrop was the uneven hump of Fairmount Hill, as seen in this 1950 photograph. (Courtesy Valerie Chester Hoover.)

The grassy open space between O'Shaughnessy Boulevard and the Miraloma Park neighborhood is known as O'Shaughnessy Hollow and was saved from development by local activists. (Courtesy San Francisco Redevelopment Agency.)

The shopping center, situated in the flat saddle of land between Red Rock and Gold Mine Hills, was one of the first things to be constructed after development of Diamond Heights began. This view looks south down Diamond Heights Boulevard. Two of Diamond Heights' three churches are visible here; the third is on Addison Street across from Walter Hass Playground. (Courtesy San Francisco Redevelopment Agency.)

A few years later, the apartments on Gold Mine Hill (seen here in the background) had been built, and trees had been planted. (Courtesy San Francisco Redevelopment Agency.)

The shopping center was meant to be a variation on a small town's "Main Street," where residents could do all their errands at once plus stop for coffee or lunch. Today the shops are also frequented by people from nearby Noe Valley, Upper Market, Glen Park, and Miraloma Park. (Courtesy San Francisco Redevelopment Agency.)

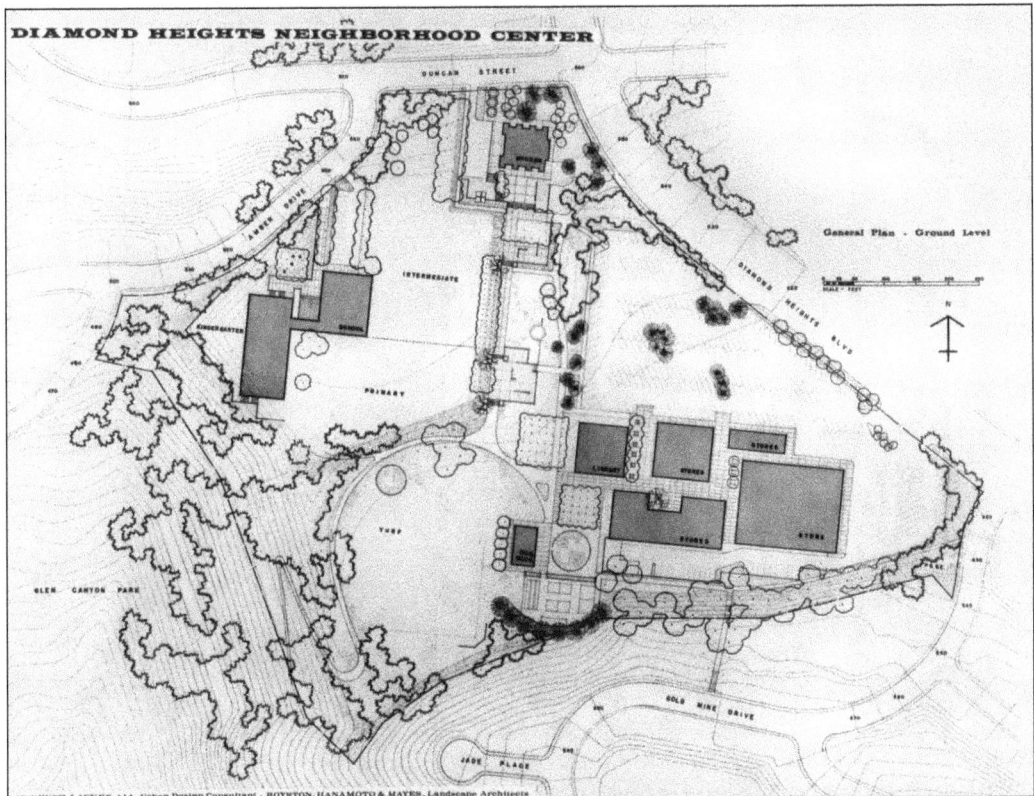

An early layout shows plans for an elementary and middle school, library (never completed), and Christopher Playground, named for George Christopher, mayor of San Francisco from 1956 to 1964. (Courtesy San Francisco Redevelopment Agency.)

Images of idyllic urban-suburban life in Diamond Heights were the focus of this marketing brochure. (Courtesy San Francisco Redevelopment Agency.)

By the 1950s, San Francisco had grown too expensive for many, and city planners hoped to coax some families to stay by building 471 units of moderately priced private housing alongside the more luxurious townhouses and condominiums on the hills. The plan, which was fairly controversial at the time, successfully integrated a variety of income levels into the Diamond Heights–Glen Park neighborhood. (Courtesy San Francisco Redevelopment Agency.)

The Diamond Heights Neighborhood Association had some say in what unfolded. The original plan called for tall residential towers, as shown in this conceptual photograph. Locals protested, though, and they were never built. (Courtesy San Francisco Redevelopment Agency.)

There was some concern among neighbors that the development would not respect the contours of the land as promised. After some debate, most of the last block of Berkeley Way, perched on the crest of Glen Canyon (Gold Mine Hill), was left undeveloped, leaving the street free for strolling and admiring the views. (Courtesy author.)

Today Diamond Heights is a mix of single-family houses, duplexes, and apartment complexes. Many of the homes are unpainted or brown-shingled, giving them a natural, woodsy look in keeping with the landscape. These impressive houses front Turquoise Way on Red Rock Hill; the photograph was taken from beneath them, on the slopes of Glen Canyon. (Courtesy private collector.)

Turquoise Way is the bottom-most street of Red Rock Hill. Amber Drive runs above it, and Quartz and Amethyst Ways run perpendicular, off to the left. At the far left of this photograph, taken from Miraloma Park and overlooking the canyon, runs Portola Drive. At its crest, Burnett Avenue begins its ascent up Twin Peaks. To the far right, one can make out St. Nicholas Orthodox Church. (Courtesy San Francisco Redevelopment Agency.)

The houses on Turquoise Way have an inspiring view of Glen Canyon Park and Mount Davidson. Today a walking path runs through the canyon just down the hill from these homes. One can access it via a public stairway that descends from Turquoise Way. (Courtesy San Francisco Redevelopment Agency.)

A sign advertising Eichler homes is visible at the top of this photograph. The construction of Diamond Heights provided opportunities for architects to stretch their wings. Joseph Eichler, probably the most famous among them, designed about 100 homes in the fledgling neighborhood. (Courtesy San Francisco Redevelopment Agency.)

Visit us at
arcadiapublishing.com